AMAZING CLAY
Flowers

Creating Realistic Flowers & Floral Arrangements

Noriko Kawaguchi

Creative Publishing
international

AMAZING CLAY
Flowers

Creative Publishing
international

First published in the United States of America in 2010

Creative Publishing International, Inc.,

A member of Quayside Publishing Group

400 First Avenue North Street

Suite 300

Minneapolis, MN 55401

1-800-328-3895

www.creativepub.com

Visit www.Craftside.Typepad.com

for a behind-the-scenes peek at our crafty world!

**Creative Publishing
international**

Copyright © 2008 Noriko Kawaguchi

Originally published in Japanese language by

Japan Broadcasting Publishing Co., Ltd.

(NHK Publishing Co., Ltd.)

English language translation & production by

World Book Media, LLC

info@worldbookmedia.com

ISBN-13: 978-1-58923-572-4

ISBN-10: 1-58923-572-X

10 9 8 7 6 5 4 3 2 1

Printed in China

CONTENTS

SPRING

SUMMER

SPRING

Cherry Blossom Light pink cherry blossoms are a hallmark of spring. The red leaves complement the delicate flowers. A single branch in a clear glass vase makes an elegant statement anywhere in the home. ❖ **Instructions on page 46**

Japanese Butterbur Before the earth has thawed, the Japanese Butterbur buds and its tiny white flowers brighten the cold ground. It's a hardy flower, and a perfect centerpiece when set in an earthen planter filled with moss. ❖ Instructions on page 38

Pansy Each tiny cluster of petals looks like a little face peeking out from amidst the greenery. Creating many flowers in different colors scatters springtime throughout the home. ❖ Instructions on page 54

Wisteria Cascading blossoms of white, purple, and violet wisteria brighten any room. In nature, it is a voracious climbing vine; in a vase, it is peaceful and lovely. ❖ **Instructions on page 59**

Anemone These lush flowers are bold statements in any arrangement. Create long- and short-stemmed blossoms (as shown) to add dimension to your bouquet. ❖ **Instructions on page 111**

Lily of the Valley These tiniest of spring flowers also have the sweetest, purest fragrance. Lily of the valley grow as abundant ground cover, and their bell-shaped blossoms ring in the season. ❖ **Instructions on page 107**

SUMMER

Lily There are as many varieties of lily as there are days of summer. This pale pink Stargazer is a fragrant, popular bloom. Experiment with any number of color combinations for a house full of lilies.

❖ **Instructions on page 92**

Thistle Do not be wary of this wildflower's prickly leaves—it is iconic, strong, and sweet. Thistle makes a striking bouquet on their own or can accent a mix of blooms. ❖ **Instructions on page 80**

Dayflower Damp with the morning dew, these tiny blue flowers unfold as the sun rises.

Nature's dayflower is fragile—it wilts as soon as the sun is high. Your handmade dayflower, however, is in perpetual bloom.

❖ **Instructions on page 72**

Chinese Lantern These distinctive flowers appear to have their own luminescence. They are delicate, paperlike, and deceptively simple to create.

❖ **Instructions on page 76**

AUTUMN

Autumn Bouquet
This colorful autumn bouquet is inspired by colorful seasonal blooms: Chrysanthemum, Balloon Flower (page 88), Japanese Dianthus, Bush Clover (page 84), Great Burnet, Eulalia (page 103) , and Stonecrop (page 105).

Eulalia Wired twine evoke this flowering grass. Use these as bouquet accents or alone as a neutral-toned centerpiece. ❖ **Instructions on page 103**

Bush Clover A branch of bush clover is dotted with tiny white, red, and purple flowers. In nature there are many varieties, and most have a very short blooming season. Some species are even endangered, which makes your handmade blossoms even more precious. ❖ Instructions on page 58

Balloon Flower From a round, white bud blooms a star-shaped purple flower. Its long, straight stem makes arranging these an exercise in minimalism.
❖ Instructions on page 88

Winter Aconite These wildflowers are in the buttercup family and they are some of the earliest bulbs to bloom as winter ends. Spring is never far away when you find these tiny shoots at your feet.

❖ Instructions on page 100

Clay Flower Bouquets

A lovely handmade bouquet can be made from any combination of flowers. Here are a few dramatic, gorgeous ideas to get you started.

Display them as part of your decor, give them as gifts, or create them for formal events, such as weddings—you are only limited by your imagination!

Old Rose Bouquet

The naturally variegated pinks and creams of these roses are elegant and lifelike. This full, traditional bouquet makes a statement as a centerpiece, or complements romantic decor. ❖ **Instructions on page 64**

BOUQUET

White Star Bouquets

The small pansy at the center of the bouquet is a surprise detail that accentuates the star-shaped flowers. This arrangement is fresh, bright, and modern. ❖ Instructions on page 114

Accessories

These dressed-up baubles add sparkle and flair to your ensembles—no one will believe they're not the real thing. For a more elegant finish, use a translucent clay base for each flower.

Anemone Pin
This creamy white anemone pin with silver stamens is a soft accent for any occasion. Pin it to a scarf, shawl, or even a handbag for a natural touch. ❖ **Instructions on page 117**

Camellia Necklace & Earrings

White camellia flowers with pearl beaded details and silver-edged leaves combine in this formal floral piece that will turn heads wherever you go. ❖ **Instructions on page 118**

Rose Basket Pin & Earrings

Miniature roses and setaria are arranged in a silver basket pin. The grasses will move with you when you wear it, as the stem of the setaria is nylon wire. ❖ **Instructions on page 121**

Materials and Tools

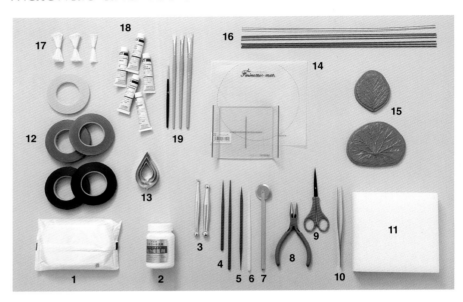

1. Resin clay (white)

The clay is used in all projects and it is easily colored with oil color. Resin clay can be easily rolled very thin, dries quickly, and is good for small detail work, making it ideal for making clay flowers. White resin clay dries translucent. (Clear resin clay dries clear.) Use small amounts of oil color to tint the clay.

2. White craft glue

Used for gluing clay pieces together, securing floral wires, and affixing jewelry findings and other components. Dab on with a paintbrush or toothpick.

3. Modeling tools with ball ends

Used for shaping flower petals. The tools and rounded ends come in several sizes. For finer curved details for petals and leaves, choose the tool with the smallest ball end.

4. Modeling stick (or stylus)

Used for shaping petals and leaves and frilling their edges. A medium-size modeling stick is used for all projects in this book, but you can experiment with different sizes.

5. + 6. Detailing tools

Additional tools can manipulate, shape, and add detail to the clay when making flowers. Use a tool with a sharp end to blend colored clays and add indentations and grooves.

7. Rolling Cutter

Used gently, a rolling cutter makes grooves and fine, straight details. Too much pressure on the roller will slice the clay.

8. Pliers

For bending, shaping, and snipping wires

9. Scissors

For cutting clay

10. Tweezers

For handling and shaping tiny detailed clay pieces

11. Foam block

Insert the stems of flowers and leaves into the foam block for drying.

12. Floral Tape

For wrapping floral wire. Floral tape comes in two widths: the smaller is used for flower petals, leaf stems, and small flowers, and the wider is used for large flowers.
The tape can also be cut in half or thirds width-wise and used for small flowers. The projects in this book use light green, brown, and mint green-colored tapes.

13. Clay cutters

Cookie-cutter-like tools used to create identical clay shapes. Press the cutter onto clay that has been rolled flat to cut multiple shapes.

14. Mini-presser and pressing mat

Sandwich the teardrop- or tube-shaped clay between the mat and the clear presser. Press until the clay is flattened in the desired size and thickness. Tip: Before pressing, apply a small amount of hand cream to the sheet so the clay releases easily.

Oil Paint Color Guide

The oil colors used to create the flowers in this book are by Holbein Artists, and can be found at most craft stores. In the project instructions we give only the generic color name (so you can match to your favorite brand's oil colors). Here is a table listing both the generic and specific color names.

Generic	Holbein Oil Color
GREEN	SAP GREEN
DARK GREEN	OXIDE CHROMIUM
GRASS GREEN	PERMANENT GREEN LIGHT
GRAY GREEN	GREEN GRAY
BLUE	ULTRAMARINE BLUE
PURPLE	MAUVE
PINK	PINK MADDER
PEONY	PEONY RED
EMPIRE RED	GERANIUM LAKE
YELLOW	PERMANENT YELLOW LIGHT
BRIGHT YELLOW	PERMANENT YELLOW DEEP
BROWN	BURNT SIENNA
DARK BROWN	BURNT UMBER
WHITE	PERMANENT WHITE
BLACK	IVORY BLACK

15. Leaf mold (strawberry and geranium styles shown)

For imprinting leaf veins in clay.

16. Floral wire

No. 14 through 28 gauge wire are used in this book. The lower the number, the thicker the wire. Thinner wire is used for flowers and leaf stems. Thicker wire is used for assembling the pieces.

17. Artificial stamens

For the flower centers; available in many sizes/styles (aurora, rose, small, etc.)

18. Oil colors

For mixing with resin clay to create colored clay. Oil color does not fade after the clay dries.

19. Paintbrushes

For adding color washes and details to the flowers; also used to apply glue.

Other Materials

Silver glitter: For adding sparkle (especially to the accessories on pages 118-121)

Toothpicks, bamboo skewers: For applying glue and drawing lines/imprints in the clay.

Plastic wrap: For protecting clay from drying out; used as a palette for oil colors

Tissue paper: For protecting the work surface while flowers and leaves dry

Aluminum foil: Use foil to create a surface or vessel for drying the clay

Starch: For making "pollen" (see Lily, page 92)

Hand cream: For lubricating your hands and the presser mat when shaping clay

Hemp thread or twine: For the tips of some grasses (see Eulalia, page 103) and flower centers (see Cyclamen, page 69).

Template-making materials: Cut templates from thick tracing paper or a plastic folder.

Basic Clay Techniques

How to Work with Resin Clay

The dimensions given in this section are approximate and are meant as guidelines.

Handling Resin Clay

- Wash your hands before working with resin clay—the clay absorbs dirt easily.
- Resin clay shrinks when it dries.
- Wrap the clay with plastic wrap when you are not working with it to prevent drying.
- Wrap the leftover clay with plastic wrap, drape a wet cloth over it, then place it in a plastic bag for storage.

Mixing Colors

Soften the unwrapped clay with your hands. Shape a ball to the desired size and make a small hollow at the center with a finger. Place a drop of oil color in the hollow and wrap the clay around it, trying not to touch the oil color with your fingers. Knead the clay until the color is even.

When clay dries, moisture evaporates and its color will darken. Add the color little by little and make the moist clay lighter than the finished product should be.

Wrapping Tape around Wire

Angle the wire against the tip of the floral tape. Wrap the wire all the way to the bottom edge. Tear it off at the end.

Making Wire Hooks

Hooked wire is inserted into the center of the flower so it does not slip out. With pliers, bend the tip of the wire ¼" (0.5 cm) down. Tighten the wire fold with pliers. This is called hooking.

Thickening the Stem (or Branch)

Some flowers require thicker stems and branches. Tear tissue paper into 1½" (4 cm) strips, fold them in half lengthwise, and wrap them around the wire. Cover the tissue with tape. Repeat this as often as needed to thicken the stem.

Smoothing the Stems

Rub the taped wire with the smooth side of the pliers to shine and burnish the tape. (This process is used for the stem of the Cyclamen [page 69] and the Anemone [page 111].)

Shaping Clay

For projects with several identical flowers and leaves, start with several identical-sized balls of clay. First, roll the clay balls in your palm in various tear-drop shapes, according to the flower and leaf instructions.

Cutting the Shaped Clay

Cut the clay into equal-sized sections (for each flower or calyx) with scissors. The depth of the cut, number of cuts, or which side to cut (wide or pointed end) differs by the flower.

For 12 equal pieces: Cut in half at pointed end, then cut each half into half, then each section into thirds.

For 5 equal pieces: Cut a one-third section from the wide end. Cut the small section in half and cut the larger section in thirds.

Create the Flower Shape

Separate each piece with a modeling tool. Shape each petal, rolling the tool left to right, into a petal shape. Thin the edges.

Pressing the Clay

Place teardrop- or tube-shaped clay on the pressing mat and flatten it into various sizes with the pressing plate.

Rub the clay with your finger where you want it to be even thinner. This shaping technique is used for both leaves and petals.

Molding the Leaf Veins

Pressed the clay against the leaf mold to create imprints of the leaf veins. An actual leaf can also be used if you cannot find a leaf mold.

Frilling

Place the pressed clay against your index finger. Add frills to the edges by rolling the modeling stick. This adds natural detail to clay flower shapes.

Rounding the Petals

Round the center of petals or edges using a modeling stick with ball ends. This also adds natural detail to clay flower shapes.

Adding Lines and Details

Add lines and details to leaves with the rolling cutter. Be careful not to apply too much pressure to the clay so you do not slice it.

Affixing the Wire

Apply glue to one-third of the wire and affix to the leaf's center vein. Pinch the clay gently around the wire.

Drying the Clay

To create a tissue paper support for drying clay: tear 2" (5 cm) -wide strips from the tissue. Fold them in half lengthwise and twist slightly to make a ring. Petals and leaves can be draped over the support so they keep their shape.

To create a curved drying surface: place layers of tissue paper and plastic wrap on a square of aluminum foil with the edges gently curved upwards. Poke wire flower stems through the center of the foil and lay the bottom of the flower against the curved surface. Place the flower in a vase to dry. This way a curved flower will hold its shape.

Foam block—For small flower and buds, insert the wires into the foam block to dry. Bend the wire so the flower faces downward and prevents the flower petals from spreading too much. For larger parts, such as leaves, layer tissue paper over the foam and drape the tips of the leaves over the edge of the block.

Coloring the Dry Clay

After the clay dries, paint it with oil color. Place the oil color(s) on the plastic wrap and mix them until you have the desired color(s). Paint a base coat then add details. Be sure to spread the color in a thin layer.

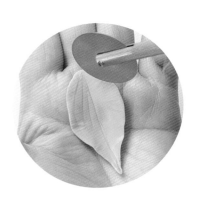

INSTRUCTIONS

SPRING

Japanese Butterbur

Resin clay

Flower: ¾" (2 cm) -diameter ball
buds, leaves: 2" (5 cm) -diameter ball

Floral wire:
No. 28 12" (30 cm): flowers and bud stems
No. 26 5" (12 cm): leaf stems
No.18 1" (2.5 cm): bud stems

Floral tape: light green (narrow): various pieces

Oil paint: white, green, grass green

Additional Materials (for arranging):
Shallow planter
Modeling clay
Foam block (cut to fit inside pot)
Dry moss
No. 20 floral wire, 1" (2.5 cm)
Dried leaves (optional)

Prepare the clay

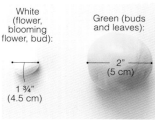

White
(flower,
blooming
flower, bud):

1 ¾"
(4.5 cm)

Green (buds
and leaves):

2"
(5 cm)

For the flowers, add a drop of white oil color to make a white clay.
For the buds and leaves, add small amounts of grass green and green oil color to tint the green clay.

1. Make the flowers

1. Cut the No. 28 wire into four equal pieces. Make a hook at one end of each piece (see page 34). Prepare forty-five hooks in the same manner. These will become the stems.

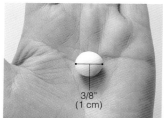 

3/8"
(1 cm)

2. Roll a ⅜" (1 cm) -diameter ball of white clay between your palms and shape it into a 2" (5 cm) long thin tube.

  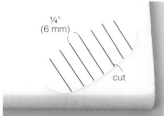

3. Place the clay on the pressing mat and flatten it with the pressing plate. Make the clay even thinner by rubbing the edge of the pressing plate across it. The clay should be about ⅛" (3 cm) thick.

4. Let the clay dry on the foam block. Trim and discard the rounded ends, and cut the clay into ¼" (6 mm) -wide strips.

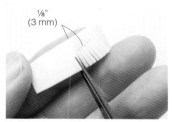 

5. Take one of the strips and cut a row of fine fringe halfway (⅛" [3 mm]) across to the other side.

6. Flip over the fringed clay strip. Apply glue to the hook end of one wire. Wrap the clay snugly around the hook and wire.

2. Make the calyx

 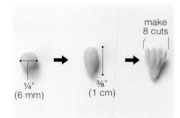  

7. Pinch the bottom of the flower so the clay is secured around the wire. Make twenty flowers using the same method. Insert them into the foam block to dry.

1. Shape a ¼" (6 mm) -diameter ball of grass green clay. Roll it between your palms to make a ⅜" (1 cm) -long teardrop. Make eight cuts into the wide end of the clay.

2. With a thin bamboo or modeling stick, make an imprint up the center of each calyx. Roll the stick between your fingers to gently spread each calyx apart. (Applying a small amount of hand cream to the bamboo prevents the moist clay from sticking to it.)

Make the calyx (continued)

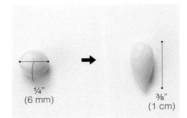

3. Insert a flower wire though the top center of the calyx. Apply glue to the bottom of the flower and press the calyx in place around it. Repeat for all twenty flowers. Insert the flowers into the foam block to dry.

3. Make the buds

1. Shape a ¼" (6 mm) -diameter ball of grass green clay. Roll it between your palms to make a ⅜" (1 cm) -long teardrop.

2. Cut the wide end of the teardrop in half. Then cut each half in half to make four equal petals. Cut each petal in half again to make eight equal petals. Then spread the petals apart slightly using the bamboo stick

glue

3. Apply glue to the hook of the stem wire, then insert the wire from the top of the bud. Pull the wire through, stopping at the hook. Gently pinch the tips of the bud closed. Make twenty-five buds and insert them into the foam block to dry.

Let the flowers and buds dry completely on the foam block.

4. Make the bud centers

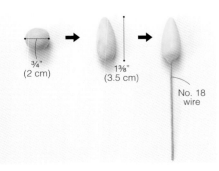

¾"
(2 cm)

1⅜"
(3.5 cm)

No. 18
wire

Wrap the No.18 wire with light green floral tape and cut it into four equal pieces. Make hooks in one end of each piece. Shape a ¾" (2 cm) -diameter ball of grass green clay. Roll it into a 1⅜" (3.5 cm)-long teardrop. Apply glue to the hook and insert the wire through the bottom of the teardrop. Spread some clay down from the teardrop base to secure it to the wire. Make four. Insert the wires into the foam block to dry.

5. Make the leaves
(*Note: The instructions are for twenty-eight leaves in three sizes: small, medium, and large.*)

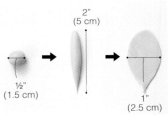

2"
(5 cm)

½"
(1.5 cm)

1"
(2.5 cm)

1. Cut twenty-eight 5" (12 cm) lengths of No. 26 wire. Do not make a hook at the end.

2. Shape a ½" (1.5 cm) -diameter ball of grass green clay. Roll it between your palms to make a 2" (5 cm) -long teardrop. Press the clay flat on the pressing mat until it is 1" (2.5 cm) wide. Work from the center of the leaf outward. Shape the edges gently with your fingers.

3. Drape the leaf over the first two fingers of the non-working hand. Roll a modeling tool along the edges of the leaf to add contour.

4. Turn the leaf over and note the visible fingerprints. This will be the top side of the leaf. Pinch the base of the leaf from below to slightly fold it.

5. Place the leaf in your palm. Roll the modeling tool with ball ends near the center of the leaf to round the sides of the leaf.

6. Gently draw fine lines in the leaf surface with the rolling cutter. First draw a line up the center from base to tip, then draw three shorter lines to the left and right of the center line.

Make the leaves (continued)

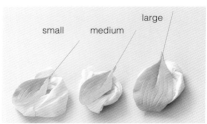

7. Apply glue to one end of the wire (from step 1). Set it along the leaf's center line, one-third of the length up from the base. Pinch the clay around the wire from below to hide the wire.

8. Make twenty-eight leaves, in small, medium, and large sizes. Add more frilly contours to the large leaves to create movement. Let each leaf dry on small twisted pieces of tissue paper.

6. Finish the buds

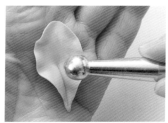

1. Follow steps 2 and 3 from step 5. Pinch the base of each leaf. Roll the modeling tool at the center of each leaf to round them.

2. Turn the leaves over and with the rolling cutter, draw lines down the leaf center and three on each side of the center line. Do the same to the other leaf.

3. While the leaves are still pliable, apply glue around the inside edges.

4. Wrap one leaf around one of the buds. Press and shape the leaf to the bud with your fingers.

5. Wrap the bud with the second leaf and press into place.

6. Make six medium leaves, following steps 1 and 2 above. Apply glue to only the lower two-thirds of the outside edges. Wrap three leaves, one at a time, around the bud. Place the leaves slightly below the small ones on the wire base.

7. Wrap the remaining three leaves around the bud, placing them slightly lower still. Reshape the tips of the leaves so that they bend out slightly. Insert the buds in the foam block and let them dry.

7. Paint the flowers

grass green   dark green   white

1. Place a small amount of each color shown on a plastic-wrapped paint palette or work surface.

2. Lightly color the tip of the flower with white.

3. Add a touch of dark green to the grass green and color the base of the calyx. Color the buds as well.

4. Add a light coat of green to the bottom of the flower and bud.

5. Mix a little dark green with grass green to make a base coat for the top of each leaf. Then lightly color the lower half of the leaf with the darker green.

6. Add white highlights along the edge of the top half of the leaf and tip of the bud.

7. Add the base coat (from step 5) to both sides of the leaves around the buds. Color the deepest bases of the leaves a dark green and highlight the tips with white.

8. Assemble the flowers

(Note: Tape refers to floral tape.)

¼" (6 mm) — No. 18 wire

1. Wrap the narrow light green tape around the No. 18 floral wire. Cut the wire into four equal pieces. Gather three flowers and wrap them together with tape, leaving ¼" (6 mm) below the flowers untaped. Align one end of the wrapped No. 18 wire to the point where the tape ends below the flowers. Tape the flowers and wire together.

2. Place five flowers around the cluster from step 1. Wrap all wires with the tape, starting just below the tape line. Always start to wrap the tape in a new place in each step to keep the stems smooth.

3. Add five more flowers to the growing flower and tape them in place. Repeat the above steps until you have assembled up to twenty flowers.

4. Place four small leaves around the flower cluster and wrap the stems with tape.

5. Arrange four medium leaves between the small leaves and wrap the stems with tape.

6. Arrange four large leaves around the flower cluster and wrap the stems with tape. Wrap all stems with one more layer of tape to create a smooth exterior and add stability.

7. Repeat steps 1-6 to create clusters of ten and fifteen buds.

8. Place eight small leaves around each bud cluster and wrap the stems with tape. Wrap all stems with one more layer of tape to create a smooth exterior and add stability.

9. Arrange the flowers

1. Cut a foam block to fit inside the planter, half the planter's depth. Place the foam at the bottom of the planter. Cut the No. 20 wire in half and shape it in a U. Insert the U through the middle of the foam so the ends poke out from the bottom of the planter. Bend the wires to the outside to secure the foam in place.

2. Fill the planter with modeling clay. Trim and shape the stems of each of the flowers and buds to create a pleasant arrangement in the clay.

3. Apply a few dots of glue to the clay surface and layer some dry moss over the clay as ground cover. Place a few decorative dry leaves on the moss.

SPRING

Cherry Blossom

Prepare the clay

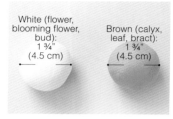

White (flower, blooming flower, bud): 1 ¾" (4.5 cm)

Brown (calyx, leaf, bract): 1 ¾" (4.5 cm)

For the flowers, tint the white clay with a small amount of pink clay. For the leaves, tint the white clay with brown clay.

MATERIALS

Resin clay:
Flower, blooming flower, bud: 1 ¾" (4.5 cm) -diameter ball
leaf, calyx, bract: 1 ¾" (4.5 cm) -diameter ball

Floral wire:
No. 24 5 ¼" (13 cm): flower stem
No. 26 2 ½" (6 cm): leaf stem
No. 18 ⅜" (1 cm): small branch
No. 14 2" (5 cm): branch

Floral tape: Light green (narrow): flower, leaf stem brown (wide): branches

Faux flower stamens (or floral pips): 3 packages/bunches

Oil paint: pink, brown, yellow, light green, purple, white

Tissue paper

1. Make the flower center (stamens)

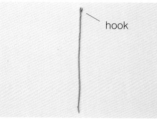

hook

1. Wrap the No. 24 wire with light green tape and cut it into four equal pieces. Make a hook at one end. Prepare fifty-two hooks in the same manner.

2. Paint the tips of the faux flower stamens (or floral pips) yellow and let them dry.

3. Take twelve of the stamens and apply glue ⅜" (1 cm) from each end. Let the glue dry, then cut the stamens in half.

4. Apply glue to the hook from step 1, and affix two clusters of stamens from step 2.

5. Wrap the base of the stamens with light green floral tape two or three times to secure.

6. Spread the stamens, making a fan-like shape. Make thirty-two flower centers.

2. Make the flowers

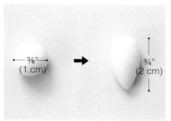

1. To make an open flower: Roll a ½" (1.5 cm) -diameter whitish-pink clay ball between your palms and shape it into a ¾" (2 cm) -long teardrop.

2. At the wide end, make a deep cut two-thirds from the outside of the teardrop. Cut the clay all the way through.

3. Cut the larger side in thirds and the smaller side in half. There are now five equal pieces.

4. With the modeling tool, gently separate each piece, rolling the tool to spread the clay into petals.

5. Snip a small V shape from the tip of each petal. Roll the modeling tool across the petal tips to spread and shape them more.

6. Leave the tips of the petals smooth, but use a square modeling tool to imprint lines at the flower center.

7. Cut the clay between the petals to separate them further.

8. Insert the flower center into the flower so the stamens are surrounded by the petals. Apply glue inside the flower. Pull the wire through so the flower center is secured.

9. Make a circle with your thumb and index finger. Wrap them gently at the back of the flower to shape the flower.

10. Bend the wire so the flower faces down. Insert it into the foam block and let it dry. Repeat steps 1-10 to make twenty-six open flowers.

11. To make a blooming flower: start with a slightly smaller flower center than the ones deacribed in steps 1-3. Overlap each of the petals instead of separating and shaping them to make smaller, tighter buds. Let them dry.

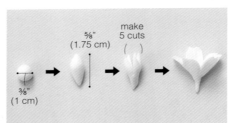

12. Make a flowering bud (without a flower center): Shape a ⅜" (1 cm) -diameter whitish-pink ball of clay into a ⅝" (1.75 cm) -long teardrop. Follow steps 4-7 to create the petals.

13. Gather the petals together so they are closed around the center of the flower. Apply glue to the hook of the wire from step 1 and insert into the bottom. Pinch the clay around the wire. Make eight buds and let them dry.

3. Make the calyx

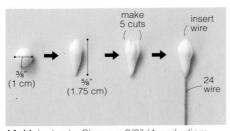

14. Make buds: Shape a 3/8" (1 cm) -diameter whitish-pink ball of clay into a 5/8" (1.75 cm) -long teardrop. Cut the wide end into five equal sections and reseal them with your fingers. Apply glue to the hook of the wire from step 1 and insert into the bottom. Make twelve buds and let them dry.

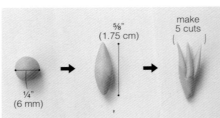

1. Shape a ¼" (6 mm) -diameter brown ball of clay into a teardrop. Roll each end into a point. Make five deep cuts in one end and spread each piece apart with a modeling tool.

bud

blooming flowers

2. Insert the wire of a finished open flower into the center of the calyx. Apply glue to the bottom of the flower and secure the calyx. Be sure that each calyx tip is aligned between two petals.

3. Flowers that have lost their petals can be made by inserting a flower center into the calyx. Make two.

4. Add a calyx to the blooming flowers and buds following steps 1-2. Let them dry in a foam block.

4. Make the leaves

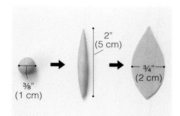

2" (5 cm)
3/8" (1 cm)
3/4" (2 cm)

1. Wrap the No. 26 wire with light green tape and cut it into four equal pieces. Make twenty-one of them.

2. Make a large leaf: Shape a 3/8" (1 cm) -diameter brown ball of clay into a 2" (5 cm) -long teardrop. Press it flat, so it is 3/4" (2 cm) wide. Working gently with your finger, press the edges thinner.

3. Place the clay on a leaf mold and press gently with your finger to imprint the leaf veins into the clay.

4. With the veined side against your index finger, roll the modeling tool along the smooth side to add texture to the edge of the leaf.

small   medium   large

5. Apply glue to a taped wire from step 1 and place it at the leaf's center vein. Pinch the wire from the back side to secure the wire against the leaf. Make seven and let them dry.

6. Make medium and small leaves by starting with smaller balls of clay. Make seven of each size. Let them dry.

5. Paint the flowers

1. Place a small amount of each color shown on a plastic-wrapped paint palette or work surface.

2. Add color to open and blooming flowers: Mix white and pink to make light pink. Paint a base coat on the front of the petals, and add a thin coat of color to the back of the petals.

3. Add a touch of light green to the center of the petals.

4. Add pink details and shading to the tips of two or three petals.

5. Add purple to a a few petal edges. Color the tips of the stamens with a brown-purple blend. Do the same on the flowers without petals.

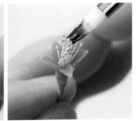

6. For the buds, paint a light pink base coat as in step 2. Color the tip of the bud lightly with a pink-purple blend.

7. Color the calyx with a purple-brown blend, brushing from bottom to top. Repeat for all flower's calyxes.

8. Paint a brown base coat on the surface of the leaf. Color lightly on the back side. Mix purple and brown and add subtle shading details to the bottom half of the leaf.

6. Make the blossom clusters (bracts)

1. Assembling the flowers: Gather four open flowers, two blooming flowers, and two buds. Align them together and wrap them once with light green tape, 1½" (3.75 cm) from the bottom of the calyxes. Wrap the stems all the way to the bottom, tape on the bias.

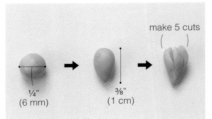

make 5 cuts

¼" (6 mm)   ⅜" (1 cm)

2. Make the bract: Shape a ¼" (6 mm) -diameter brown ball of clay into a ⅜" (1 cm) -long teardrop. Cut the wide end into five equal pieces.

3. Spread each section apart with the modeling tool. Make a hole at the center.

4. Insert the flower stem made in step 1 into the bract. Apply glue at the top of the tape and secure the bract to the stem.

5. Assemble the remaining flowers and buds into six clusters, placing six to nine flowers in each. Let dry, then color them the same as the calyx in step 7 above.

6. Gather three leaves: a large leaf at the center and the small and medium leaves to the right and left, and 1" (2.5 cm) below the bottom of the large leaf. Wrap the wires once with the light green tape, then wrap the steps to the bottom, tape on the bias. Make seven sets. Make bracts for the leaves and color them the same as the calyx in step 7 above.

7. Make the branches

1. Make a shoot: Cut a 3 ⅛" (7.75 cm) -long piece of brown tape. Pull the tape slightly to stretch it. Fold it in half, then fold the end on a diagonal.

2. Roll the shoot by wrapping the long ends around the fold, which becomes the core. Squeeze the bottom to pinch it closed. Make eight.

2" (5 cm)

3. Make small branches: Wrap the No. 18 wire with brown tape and cut it into four equal sections. Tear tissue paper into 1⅝" (4 cm) -wide strips. Fold in thirds and wrap it around the wire.

4. Place the tip of the small branch in the center of the floral tape end and wrap the small branch on the bias down to the bottom.

8. Assemble the Cherry Blossom

*Use brown tape for flower stems *Wrap tissue paper or tapes around thin branches to thicken them, giving the finished Cherry Blossom stems and branches a more natural appearance. *The flowers, leaves, small branches, and shoots can be assembled in any order.

Wrap the No. 14 wire with tape

1. Make the large branch: Wrap the No. 14 wire with tape. Place the bottom of a flower cluster (bract) against the branch and wrap with the tape for 2" (5 cm) to secure the two together. Cut the tape.

2. Place the leaf section 2" (5 cm) below the flower cluster against the branch. Wrap with the tape for 2" (5 cm). Cut the tape. Repeat for two more flower clusters and one more leaf section.

3. Place another flower cluster 2" (5 cm) below the leaf parts attached in step 2. Wrap the length of the branch with tape, adjusting the shoots, small branch, and leaves. Bend and shape the branch with your hands.

AMAZING CLAY FLOWERS

4. Make the side branch: Wrap the entire length of the No. 14 wire with brown tape. Double wrap the top 2" (5 cm). Leave a few small branches bare, place the leaves and wrap them with tape. Place two buds (not aligned) together and tape them in place, facing each other. Place the flowers 2" (5 cm) below it.

5. Continue to place on the large branch (in order) a leaf, flower, leaf, flower, leaf, and small branch, and tape them in place. Wrap tissue paper around the thin branches to thicken them.

6. Bring the two branches together without aligning the flowers. Wrap twice tightly with tape to finish the Cherry Blossom.

SPRING

Pansy

MATERIALS (for five bunches)

Resin clay:
Bud, inner petal: 1" (2.5) ball
Bud, outer petal: 1" (2.5) ball
Calyx, leaf: 1⅝" (4 cm) ball

Floral wire:
No. 26 2" (5 cm): small leaf stem
No. 24 4" (10 cm): medium and large leaf stem
No. 22 ¾" (2 cm): half-open flower stem
No. 20 1¼" (3 cm): flower stems

Floral tape: Light green (narrow)

Oil paint: green, dark green, grass green, blue, purple, empire red, yellow, bright yellow, white

*Note: Instructions are for one bunch.

Prepare the clay

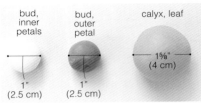

For the inner petals of the buds, add a tiny amount of yellow to the clay to make it creamier.

For the outer petals of the buds, add a tiny amount of purple and blue to to the clay to make it a richer purple.

For the calyx and leaf, add a tiny amount of green and dark green to the clay to make it darker green.

1. Make the inner petals

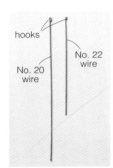

1. Prepare wire stems for one bunch. For the open flower stems, wrap No. 20 wire with narrow floral tape. Cut the wire in half and make a hook at one end. Prepare one. For the bud stems, wrap No. 22 wire with the floral tape. Cut in thirds and make a hook at one end. Prepare one.

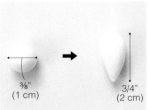

2. Shape the ⅜" (1 cm) ball of white clay into a ¾" (2 cm) -long teardrop.

3. Cut the wide end of the teardrop in two so there are two unevenly shaped halves. Cut the smaller half of the teardrop in half again.

4. Roll the modeling tool across the petals vertically to make frilled edges and to spread the clay thinner.

5. Cut between the petals to separate them.

6. Pull the base of the large petal over the edges of the small petals, and overlap the two small petals slightly.

7. Insert a piece of No. 20 wire (from step 1) through the center of the petals. Apply glue just under the hook and affix it to the clay. Pull the wire gently until just the tip of the wire is visible. The hook will be the flower center. Use the tip of a scissor blade to draw lines at the flower center. Let it dry in the foam block.

2. Make the outer petals

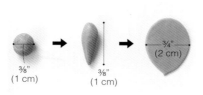

top

1. Shape a ⅜" (1 cm) ball of purple clay into a ¾" (2 cm) -long teardrop. Press the clay flat on the pressing mat until it is ¾" (2 cm) wide. Stretch the petal's edges with your finger to make it thinner.

2. Leaving the lower half of the petal flat, frill the edges with a modeling tool. The side with visible finger-prints will be the top. Make three.

Make outer petals *(continued)*

back

3. Apply glue to the bases of two petals from step 2 and affix them to the back of the white inner petals. The two outer petals should overlap each other. This is the open flower. Let it dry in the foam block.

3. Make the bud

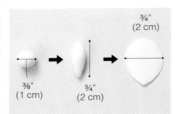   

1. Shape a ⅜" (1 cm) ball of cream-colored clay into a ¾" (2 cm) -long teardrop. Press the clay flat on the pressing mat until it is ¾" (2 cm) wide. Stretch the petal's top half with your finger to make it thinner but leave the lower half untouched.

2. Let the wider half curl in on itself. Apply glue to the hook of a No. 22 stem wire. Insert wire through the open, curled petal. Pinch the bottom of the petal to close it. This will be a bud.

3. Make the outer petal from purple clay to the same size as the petals from step 1. Frill the edges.

4. Apply glue to the inside of the third purple petal and wrap it around the bud. Let the bud dry completely in the foam block.

4. Make the calyx

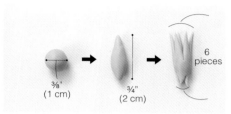

1. Shape a ⅜" (1 cm) ball of green clay into a ¾" (2 cm) -long teardop (with both ends pointed). Cut each end in six equal pieces. Cut to the middle from the top and cut just slightly from the bottom.

2. Separate and spread each piece with the modeling tool.

3. Apply glue to the bottom of the open flower. Insert the wire stem through the calyx and affix it to the bottom of the flower. With the modeling tool, create an indentation around the lower-middle calyx. Repeat this step for the bud.

5. Make the leaves

Prepare wire stems for one bunch: For a small leaf: wrap No. 26 wire with narrow floral tape and cut in four. Prepare four. For medium and large leaf: wrap No. 24 wire with narrow floral tape and cut in three. Prepare five.

Dimensions for two sizes of leaves are listed: small and large. Use a size between the two for medium-size leaves.

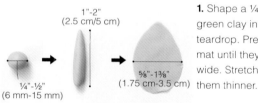

1. Shape a ¼"/½" (6 mm/15 mm) ball of green clay into a 1"/2" (2.5 cm/5 cm) -long teardrop. Press the clay flat on the pressing mat until they are ⅝"/1⅜" (1.75 cm/ 3.5 cm) wide. Stretch the edges of the leaves to make them thinner.

2. Place one leaf on the strawberry leaf mold. Gently press with your finger to imprint the leaf veins in the clay.

3. Cut a small V shape at the base of the leaf.

4. Turn the leaf over. Roll the modeling tool along the edges of the leaf to make frills. Press a bamboo stick into the edge of the leaf every ¼" (6 mm) to create tiny waves or teeth.

5. Apply glue to the tip of the stem wire. Set it along the leaf's center line, one-third of the length up from the base. Pinch the clay around the wire from below to hide it. Make nine leaves total in three sizes (small, medium and large). Insert them into the foam block to dry.

6. Paint the flowers and leaves

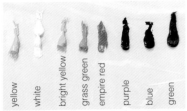

1. Place a small amount of each color shown on a plastic-wrapped paint palette or work surface.

2. Mix white and yellow to make a pale yellow. Add a base coat of the yellow to the inner petals. Paint a purple base coat on both sides of the outer petals. Paint pale yellow and bright yellow details around the center of the inner petals.

3. Mix empire red and bright yellow to make orange. Paint around the center of the inner petal. With a thin paintbrush and a mixed blue-purple paint, paint lines that radiate from the center. Paint three lines each on the upper petals and seven on the lower one.

4. Add grass green details at the flower center, yellow below it, and white above it. Paint the corner of the outer petal with mixed blue-purple, and paint the lower part of the inner petal (a small triangle) with the same color. Add white highlights at the corner of the outer petal.

5. Paint a base coat of purple on the bud. Paint the inside of the flower with mixed blue-purple. Add white highlights to the corner of the petals.

6. Paint a base coat of mixed green and grass green on the calyx. Paint the edges with white. With pliers, bend the wire at the base of the calyx in a 90 degree angle. Repeat with the bud.

7. Paint a base coat of mixed green and grass green on the leaf. Lightly coat the backside but add a darker coat of green at the center of the leaf. Paint a thin white line up the center leaf vein, even narrower at the tip.

7. Assemble the flower

1. Align the wire of the bud about 3" (7.5 cm) below the bottom of the calyx of the open flower. Wrap the stems a few times with floral tape.

2. Arrange the stems of four small leaves around the flower and bud. Letting about 1⅝" (4 cm) of the leaf stems remain visible, wrap the stems with floral tape. Arrange the medium and large leaves around the growing bunch. Letting about 2" (5 cm) of the stems remain visible, wrap the steps with floral tape. Wrap the entire length of the stem once more to stabilize it. One pansy bunch is complete!

Repeat all steps to create each additional bunch. Each can have a range of different sizes and placement of leaves.

SPRING

Wisteria

MATERIALS (for two branches)

Resin clay:

Flower center: 2" (5 cm) ball
Inner petal: 2" (5 cm) ball
Bud/outer petal: 2¾" (7 cm) ball
Calyx/leaf: 1⅝" (4 cm) ball

Floral wire:

No. 26 8 ¼" (21 cm): bud, leaf stem
No. 24 5¼" (13 cm): flower center stem
No. 20 ¾" (2 cm): for assembling flower
No. 18 1½" (4 cm): for assembling leaf
No. 14 ¾" (2 cm): branch

Floral tape

light green (narrow and regular width)
brown

Oil paint: green, grass green, purple, blue, yellow, bright
yellow, brown, white

Prepare the clay

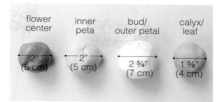

For the flower center, mix small amounts of purple
and blue to make a 2" (5 cm) lilac clay ball.
For the Inner petal, mix slight amounts of purple and
blue to make a 2" (5 cm) pale lavender clay ball.
For the bud/outer petal, mix just a trace of blue to give
the 2¾" (7 cm) white clay ball a bluish under-tone.
For the calyx/leaf, mix small amounts of green and
brown to make a 1⅝" (4 cm) leafy green clay ball.

1. Make flower centers and buds

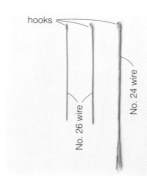

1. Prepare the floral wires. For the
small buds, cut the No. 26 wire into
six equal pieces. Make a hook at one
end of each piece. Make forty pieces.
For the buds, wrap the No. 26 wire
with narrow floral tape and cut into six
equal pieces. Make a hook at one end
of each piece. Make 30. For the flower
center, wrap the No. 24 wire with narrow floral tape and cut into four equal
pieces. Make a hook at one end of
each piece. Make 50.

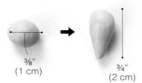

2. Make the flower center. Roll a ⅜"
(1 cm) ball of lilac clay between your
palms and shape it into a ¾" (2 cm)
long teardrop.

Make flower centers and buds *(continued)*

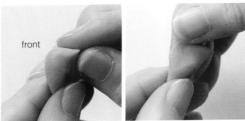

3. Pinch the top of the clay to make a horn-like shape. Also, pinch the front of the clay to make it thinner.

4. Apply glue to the hook of a No. 24 wire and insert it into the bottom of the flower center from step 3. Pinch the bottom of the bud center to secure it to the wire. Make a total of fifty flower centers in the same manner, in varying sizes. Insert them into the foam block to dry.

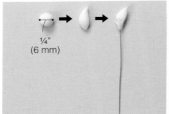

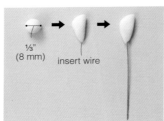

5. Make the small buds. Roll a ¼" (6 mm) white clay ball between your palms and shape it into a ⅝" (1.75 cm) -long teardrop. Curve the left side slightly and the tip so that it comes to a sharp point. Insert a piece of No. 26 wire (without tape) into the base of the clay. Make three small cuts in the base to make the calyx. Make forty total, in varying sizes.

6. Make the bud. Roll a ⅓" (8 mm) white clay ball in to a ¾" (2 cm) -long teardrop. Pinch the top of the teardrop to flatten it and shape the base so that it comes to a a flat, sharp point. Apply glue to the hook of a No. 26 wire and insert into the bottom of the bud. Pinch to secure it. Make thirty total, in varying sizes.

2. Make the inner petals

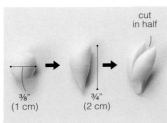

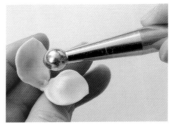

1. Roll a ⅜" (1 cm) pale lavender clay ball in to a ¾" (2 cm) -long teardrop. Pinch the top to sharpen it, then cut it in half. Spread the two halves with a modeling tool. Roll the tool across the bottom half of the inner petal to widen it.

2. Roll the ball-end tool across the petal center to create a rounded shape.

3. Apply glue to the bottom of the flower center. Insert it between the two petals. Pinch the base of the inner petals to secure them to the center. Make fifty.

4. Insert them into the foam block, bending the wire so the petals face downward, and let them dry.

3. Make the outer petals

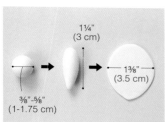  

1. Roll a 3/8"-5/8" (1-1.75 cm) white clay ball into a 1¼" (3 cm) -long teardrop. Place the clay on the pressing mat and flatten it with the pressing plate until it is 3/8" (1 cm) wide. Stretch the edges with your fingers to make it thinner.

2. Roll the ball-end modeling tool along the edges to make frills. Turn it over. Gently press a scissor blade along the center of the petal to make an imprint.

3. Fold the petal in half along the line. Pinch the petal from behind to shape it.

4. Apply glue to the bottom of the petal and wrap it around the base of the inner petal. Make fifty outer petals, all in slightly different shapes. Repeat this step with all inner petals. Let the petals dry in the foam block.

4. Make the calyx

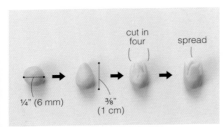

1. Roll a ¼" (6 mm) leafy green ball into a to ⅜" (1 cm) -long pear shape. Cut the top end into four. Spread the four pieces apart with a modeling tool. This is the calyx.

2. Insert the petals and bud into the calyx from the top so the wire pokes through the center of the calyx. Apply glue to the base and pinch the clay to secure it. Let dry in the foam block.

5. Make the leaves

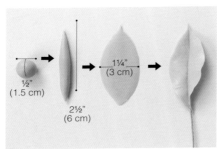

Wrap a length of No. 26 wire with narrow tape and cut it into six equal pieces. Shape a ½" (1.5 cm) ball of leafy green clay into a long, thin, sharpened teardrop. Place the clay on the pressing mat and flatten it with the pressing plate until it is 1¼" (3 cm). Stretch the edges with your fingers to make it thinner. Place one leaf on the strawberry leaf mold. Gently press with your finger to imprint the leaf veins in the clay. Glue the wire at the center of the leaf.

6. Paint the flowers

Place a small amount of each color shown on a plastic-wrapped paint palette or work surface.

1. Mix purple, blue, and white to make a pale lilac basecoat for the outer petal, bud, and small bud. Next, mix purple and a hint of blue to make a purple basecoat for the inner petal and flower center. Mix purple and slightly more blue to add highlights and detail to the flower center and the inner petal.

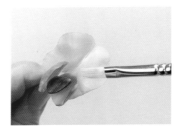

2. Using same brush, paint the edges of the outer petal. Next, paint the outer petal center with white.

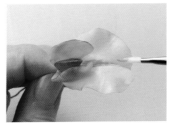

3. On top of the white paint from step 2, paint yellow, then add bright yellow details, too.

4. Add a basecoat of pale lilac for the small bud and bud, then lightly paint the edges with the same color used for the edges of the outer petal.

5. Mix a basecoat of grass green mixed with a touch of brown for the calyx. Paint the base of the flower brown. Repeat for the small bud and bud.

6. Mix a basecoat of grass green mixed with brown to the leaf. Lightly paint the back side of the leaf. Lightly paint the leaf center. Add brown around the edge. Repeat for all fifty-two.

7. Assemble the flowers

1. Tightly wrap the No. 18 wire with narrow floral tape and cut the wire in half. Place the wire at the base of one leaf and wrap the two wires together with tape. Place another leaf ⅝" (1.75 cm) below the previous leaf on the wire. Wrap wire two to three times with narrow tape. Place another leaf on the opposite side and wrap it with tape. Place an-other leaf 1" (2.5 cm) lower and tape it as well. Add a leaf opposite. Repeat this process until you have thirteen leaves. Make a second branch.

2. Wrap the No. 14 wire with wide brown floral tape. Wrap the top 2" (5 cm) with tape three to four times to thicken it.

3. Place one branch 2" (5 cm) down from the top end of the thick branch and wrap with brown tape for about 2" (5 cm). Wrap twice to thicken it.

4. Place the second leaf branch 2"-2½" (5-6 cm) below the first one and wrap with brown tape.

5. Arrange half the small buds, buds, and flowers around the No. 20 wire. Wrap all pieces with narrow tape. For added stability, wrap No. 18 wire along one side of the branch.

6. Join the branches from step 4 and the flower from step 5 and wrap a couple of times with wide brown tape. Wrap the entire branch once more with tape to finish. Repeat for the second branch.

BOUQUETS

Old Rose Bouquet

MATERIALS (for five bunches)

Resin clay:
Flower center, petal: 1⅝" (4 cm) ball
Calyx, leaf: 1¼" (3 cm) ball

Floral wire
No. 24 1: small leaf stems
No. 22 1: big leaf stems
No. 16 1: flower stem

Floral tape: light green (narrow)

Oil paint: green, dark green, sage green, purple, yellow, pink, white

Prepare the clay

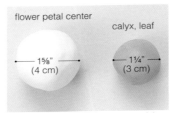

flower petal center

calyx, leaf

1⅝"
(4 cm)

1¼"
(3 cm)

For the flower petal center, add a touch of pink to a 1⅝" (4 cm) white clay ball to make pale pink.
For the calyx and leaf, add green and dark green to a 1¼" (3 cm) white clay ball to make green.

1. Make the flower center

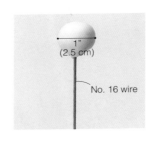

1"
(2.5 cm)

No. 16 wire

1. Wrap floral tape around the No. 16 wire and cut it in half. Make a hook at one end of each piece. Roll the pale pink clay into a 1" (2.5 cm) ball. Apply glue to the hook and insert the hook into the ball. Pinch a small amount of clay at the bottom to secure it to the wire. Let it dry in the foam block.

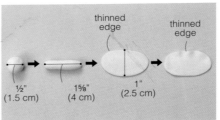

thinned
edge

thinned
edge

½"
(1.5 cm)

1⅝"
(4 cm)

1"
(2.5 cm)

2. You will now make petals to wrap around the flower center. Roll a ½" (1.5 cm) pale pink ball of clay be-tween your palms and shape it into a 1 ⅝" (4 cm) -long tube. Place the clay on the pressing mat and flatten it with the pressing plate until it is 1" (2.5 cm) wide. Stretch the upper edge with your finger to make it thinner.

½"
(1.5 cm)

3. Place the petal in the palm of your hand. Curl the petal and frill the edges with a ball-end modeling tool.

4. Apply glue to the bottom half of the petal. Place it on top of the flower center. Fold in the left side of the petal and wrap the right side around it. The petal will look like a pointed cap on the flower center.

2. Make the petals

Prepare three petals each for rows 1 through 4. The instructions are the same for each row but the sizes differ.

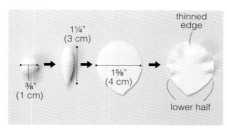

thinned edge

1¼"
(3 cm)

1⅝"
(4 cm)

⅜"
(1 cm)

lower half

1. Make the first row of petals. Roll pale pink clay into a ⅜" (1 cm) ball and shape it into a 1¼" (3 cm) -long teardrop. Place the clay on the pressing mat and flatten it with the pressing plate until it is 1⅝" (4 cm) wide. Stretch the upper edges with your finger to make them even thinner. Leave the lower half flat, but use the ball-end modeling tool to add curls and frills to the petal.

2. Holding from the back side (the top side has visible fingerprints), pinch in the middle to fold the lower half of the petal in half, creating a crease.

3. Place the petal in your palm and press with your fingers the crease you just created to flatten it out slightly.

4. Use the ball-end modeling tool to make the petal round, especially the upper half. It should look like a shallow dish.

5. From the back side, pinch the middle of a corner.

Make the petals (continued)

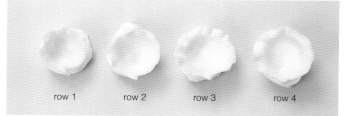

row 1   row 2   row 3   row 4

6. Bend back the upper edges slightly. Make three creases around the upper edges.

7. Place the petals on a twisted piece of tissue paper until they are half dry. Repeat above steps to create petals for layers 2 through 4. Make three petals in each size.
Layer 2: Shape a ½" (1.5 cm) ball into 1⅜" (3.5 cm) -long teardrop.
Press it flat on a pressing mat until it is 1¾" (4.5 cm) wide.
Layer 3: Shape a ⅝" (1.75 cm) ball into 1⅝" (4 cm) -long teardrop.
Press it flat on a pressing mat until it is 2" (5 cm) wide.
Layer 4: Shape a ¾" (2 cm) ball into 1⅝" (4 cm) -long teardrop.
Press it flat on a pressing mat until it is 2¼" (5.5 cm) wide.

3. Assemble the flowers

1. Apply glue to the lower corner of all twelve petals. With edges overlapping, place three petals for layer 1 around the flower center, leaving some air space. The flower should still be rounded in shape.

2. Arrange the three petals for layer 2 around the flower center, aligning them between the petals of row 1.

3. Repeat for layers 3 and 4, lowering each row slightly. Insert the flower stem into the foam block to dry.

4. Make the calyx

After the flower has dried, wrap the stem twice with narrow tape to thicken it. Burnish the tape to make the stem shiny.

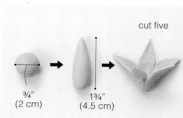

cut five

¾"
(2 cm)   1¾"
(4.5 cm)

1. Roll a ¾" (2 cm) ball of green clay into a 1¾" (4.5 cm) -long teardrop. Cut the sharper end into five equal parts. Use a modeling tool to spread the petals apart and widen each petal.

2. Place the ball-end tool at the widest part of each calyx to make them rounded. Do not spread or widen the center, only the calyx segments.

3. Make two small cuts in each side of all five petals (see photo). Make a hole through the center of the calyx with a modeling stylus.

4. Insert the flower stem through the calyx center. Apply glue to the base of the flower and secure it to the calyx. Gently press the modeling tool against the base of each calyx petal to create a curved surface. Let the flower dry in the foam block.

4. Make the leaves

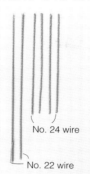

No. 24 wire

No. 22 wire

1. Wrap the No. 22 and No. 24 wires with narrow floral tape. Cut the No. 22 in three pieces; use two for the big leaves. Cut the No. 24 in four pieces, and use all four for the small leaves.

2. Pull the sides of a leaf-shaped clay cutter outward to make a rounder leaf.

3. Roll a ¾" (2 cm) ball of green clay into a 2" (5 cm) -long tear-drop. Press the clay flat on the pressing mat until it is just larger than the leaf clay cutter. Cut the leaf shape.

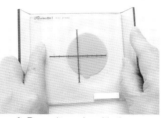

4. Press it again with the pressing mat to make the leaf larger. Stretch the corner of the leaf with your finger to make it thinner.

5. Place one leaf on the strawberry leaf mold. Gently press with your finger to imprint the leaf veins in the clay.

6. Flip the back side to the front, and roll the modeling tool along the edges to add gentle curls and frills.

7. Apply a little glue to the tip of the No. 22 wire. Affix to the center of the leaf and pinch the wire from behind to secure it. Make two (this is the large leaf). Make smaller leaves by not reflattening the clay in step 4. Affix No. 24 wire to each smaller leaf. Make four. Let the leaves dry in the foam block.

6. Paint and assemble the flowers and leaves

Place a small amount of each color shown on a plastic-wrapped paint palette or work surface.

1. Mix a base coat for the flower of pink and white. Paint the middle part of the flower pink. Over the pink, paint a layer of pink and purple mixed.

2. Mix white and yellow to make cream and paint the flower edges to add highlights.

3. Mix a base coat for the calyx of green and sage green. Paint white details at the edges of the clayx.

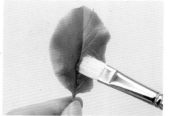

4. Mix a base coat for the leaves of green and sage green. Paint a light coat on the back side. Paint the middle of each leaf dark green.

5. Paint the center leaf vein white, brushing from the base to the tip. Repeat for all six leaves.

6. Assemble the leaves into clusters of three. The large leaf is the center and the small leaves are attached 1" (2.5 cm) below on the sides. Wrap each stem two or three times with floral tape when attaching them to the main stem. Wrap the entire stem with tape. Make another set of leaves.

7. Place one of the three-leaf clusters ¾" (2 cm) below the flower on the branch. Wrap each stem two or three times with floral tape, then wrap the entire stem to secure it. Place another three-leaf branch 3¾" (2 cm) below the first, and wrap as for the first. The leaves should all face center. Burnish the stem with the side of the pliers to make it shiny. The rose is complete.

To make the bouquet, make fourteen or fifteen of the roses. Gather them together and wrap the stems with tulle, then wrap the stems with decorative ribbon.

ꙠINTER

Clyclamen

Prepare the clay

For the open and half-open flowers, add peony to a 2⅜" (5.75 cm) white clay ball to make salmon pink.

For the bud, add a small amount of the clay from the open flower and white paint to a 1" (2.5 cm) white clay ball to make pale pink.

For the calyx and leaf, add green and dark green to a 3⅛" (7.75 cm) white clay ball to make pale green.

MATERIALS (for one pot)

Resin clay:
Open flower, half-open flower: 2⅜" (5.75 cm) ball
Bud: 1" (2.5 cm) ball
Calyx, stem: 3⅛" (7.75 cm) ball

Floral wire:
No. 18 53: half open flower, bud stem
No. 16 8: open flower stem

Floral tape
brown (narrow and regular width)

Oil paint: green, sage green, dark green, peony, purple, pink, empire red, brown, white

Hemp thread (flower center)

1. Make the calyx

hook

1. Make the stems. Wrap the No. 16 wire with the regular width brown floral tape and bend one end into a hook. Tear tissue paper into 2" (5 cm) -wide strips and fold them in thirds. Wrap the wire, starting from just below the hook and wrapping for 10" (25 cm). Wrap the tissue with the regular-width brown tape the whole length of the wire. Burnish the stem with the side of the pliers to make it shiny.

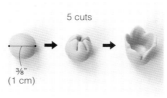

5 cuts

⅜"
(1 cm)

2. Make the calyx. Roll a ⅜" (1 cm) ball of pale green clay and make five equal cuts in the top. Insert the modeling tool at the top and roll it gently to create space between the cuts. (See page 107, Lily of the Valley, for more detailed instructions for this technique.)

3. Apply glue to the top of the hook and insert it into the bottom of the calyx. Pinch the clay around it to secure it. Reshape the calyx so it is rounded. Gently bend each petal of the calyx so they curl outward. Make eight. Insert them into the foam block to dry.

2. Make the open flower

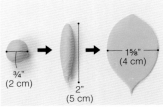

1. Roll a ¾" (2 cm) ball of salmon pink clay and shape it into a 2" (5 cm) -long teardrop. Press the clay flat on the pressing mat until it is 1⅝" (4 cm) wide. Stretch the edges of the petal with your fingers to make it thinner.

2. Roll the modeling tool along the edge to add texture and frills. Turn it over and press the edges with a stylus to add more details.

3. Make a line up the middle of the petal with a rolling cutter (center vein). Add two or three lines branching out from both sides of the center vein. Fold the petal in half from behind to shape it. Make five (for one pot). Set them on tissue until they are half dry.

5. Make the flower center. Cut twenty strands of ⅜" (1 cm) long thread. Apply glue to the base and affix them at the center of the petals. Fill the space beneath the flower petals with tissue paper so the flower keeps its shape until it dries. Make eight.

flower center

4. Apply glue to the bottom back side of each petal. Insert the base into the calyx to secure them. Bend the petal outwards and down. Glue five petals to the calyx.

3. Make the half-open flower and bud

For the stems, cut No. 18 wire into 7¾" (20 cm) -long pieces and prepare them as the calyx stems (see page 69).

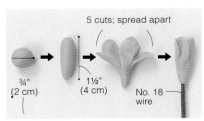
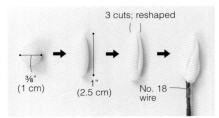

1 Make the half-open flower. Roll a ¾" (2 cm) salmon pink ball of clay and shape it into a 1½" (4 cm) -long teardrop. Cut the wider end of the clay into five equal segments. Spread each piece apart and flatten slightly with a modeling tool. Shape the bud by folding the petals back together. Apply glue to the hook of a No. 18 wire and insert it into the base of the flower. Make six.

2. Make the bud. Roll a ⅜" (1 cm) pale pink ball of clay and shape it into a 1" (2.5 cm) teardrop. Cut the thinner end of the clay into three parts, then push the clay together again. Hold the tip gently and and twist. Insert No. 18 wire into the base of the bud. Make seven.

3. Make the calyx for the bud with a ⅜" (1 cm) ball of clay, following the steps for the open flower (see page 69). Apply glue to the base of the half-open flower and bud and insert them into the calyx. Let them dry completely in the foam block.

4. Make the leaves

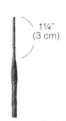

1¼"
(3 cm)

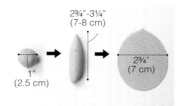

2¾"-3¼"
(7-8 cm)

1"
(2.5 cm)

2¾"
(7 cm)

1. Make the stems. Cut the No. 18 wire into 7¾" (20 cm) lengths and wrap with regular width brown tape. Leave the top 1¼" (3 cm) and wrap the rest with tissue paper and another layer of floral tape to thicken it. Make forty.

2. Make a large leaf. Roll a 1" (2.5 cm) ball of pale green clay and shape it into a 2¾"-3¼" (7-8 cm) -long teardrop. Press the clay flat on the pressing mat until it is 2¾" (7 cm) wide.

3. Cut a V into the base of the leaf. With the leaf still on the pressing mat, add jagged texture around the edges with four or five toothpicks.

4. Put it on the geranium leaf mold to copy leaf vein. Roll the tool from the back side and make frills at the corner.

5. Turn the leaf over to show the top side and cut the bottom. Apply glue on the thinner side of the wire, then attach to the center of the leaf. Pinch some clay from the back to stick them together. Make the medium leaf smaller in diameter. Make 40 total large and medium sizes.

5. Paint the flowers, buds, and leaves

Place a small amount of each color on a plastic-wrapped paint palette or work surface.

2. Apply the pink and purple base coat to the half-open flower. Shade the lower section with purple. Highlight the corner of each petal with white. Mix a base coat of mixed green and sage green for the calyx. Paint the tips white. Add a reddish hue to the base with purple mixed with brown. Mix white and pink for a base coat for the bud. Finish with white on the top and pink for the bottom.

1. Mix a pink base coat from pink and purple. Brushing from top to bottom, paint the center of each petal. Over this base coat, paint with a mix of peony and purple. Shade the center and edges of each flower with purple. Highlight the corner of each petal with white.

3. Apply a base coat of green mixed with sage green for the leaves. Paint the center with dark green and paint white brushstroke highlights. Paint the tips with purple mixed with brown.

4. After the paint has dried, bend the wire with pliers at the base of the flower so the flower faces down. Repeat with the half-open flower and the bud.

To arrange the Cyclamen, fill the pot with foam and modeling clay (as shown on page 45 of Japanese Butterbur). Insert the leaves first, then the open flower, the half-open flower, and the bud, then cover with dried moss.

SUMMER

Dayflower

Prepare the clay

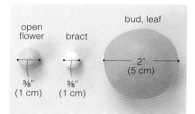

open flower

bract

bud, leaf

⅜" (1 cm)

⅜" (1 cm)

2" (5 cm)

For the open flower, add a touch of blue to a ⅜" (1 cm) ball of white clay to make blue.

For the bract, add a small amount of dark brown to a ⅜" (1 cm) ball of white clay to make a pale beige.

For the bud and leaf, add green and dark green to a 2" (5 cm) ball of white clay I to make green.

MATERIALS (for five bunches)

Resin clay:
Open flower: ⅜" (1 cm) ball
Bract: ⅜" (1 cm) ball
Bud, leaf: 2" (5 cm) bal

Floral wire:
No. 24   2: leaf stems
No. 22   1: open flower and bud stems
No. 18   1: assembling the flower

Floral tape: Light green (narrow and regular width)

Oil paint: green, dark green, sage green, grass green, blue, yellow, brown, dark brown, white, purple

Rose pips: 5 (flower center)

1. Make the open flower

* Wrap the No. 22 wire tightly with narrow floral tape and cut it in half. Make a hook at one end of one piece. This will be the flower stem.

1. Paint the tip of one pip brown. Cut it in half. Hold the two brown pips with a white one and curl the ends with the end of the modeling tool. Apply glue to the base of the pips.

2. Paint two pips yellow. Cut them in half and gather four together in a bundle. Apply glue just below the tips. Apply glue to the wire hook. Affix the pips from step 1 to the back side and the yellow pips to the front. Wrap the pips once with narrow tape. This is the flower center.

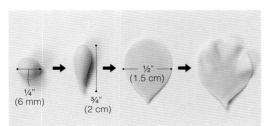

3. Roll a ¼" (6 mm) ball of blue clay between your palms and shape it into a ¾" (2 cm) -long teardrop. Place the clay on the pressing mat and flatten it until it is ½" (1.5 cm) wide. Make the top half thinner by stretching the clay with your fingers. Roll the modeling tools along the top edges to add texture. Make two. Let them dry partially.

4. Bend the wire stem slightly. Apply glue to the base of two petals and attach them to the stem, wrapping the base around the flower center from behind the yellow pips.

2. Make the bract

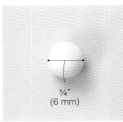

1. Roll a ¼" (6 mm) ball of pale beige clay and shape it into a ⅜" (1 cm) -long teardrop. Cut the thinner end in half and spread the halves apart with a modeling tool.

2. Insert the stem of the open flower into the center of the bract. Apply glue to the inside base to secure them.

3. Repeat step 1 to make a second two-part shape, but cut the thicker end in half instead. Insert the stem with the open flower through the center. Apply glue to the base to secure it. This covers the bract made in step 2.

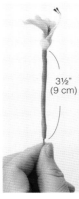

3½" (9 cm)

4. Finish the stem. Roll a ⅜" (1 cm) ball of green clay into a thin, 2" (5 cm) -long snake. Hollow the center of the snake by pushing a bamboo stick through it. Remove the clay from the bamboo. Coat the wire with glue and slip the green clay tube over the stem. (See Lily, page 92, for details instructions.) Roll the clay stem between your palms until it is 3½" (9 cm) long. Let the flower and stem dry completely.

3. Make the bud

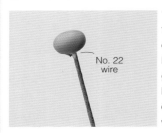

No. 22 wire

1. Wrap the No. 22 wire with narrow floral tape and cut into thirds. Make a hook at one end of one piece. This will be the stem. Roll a ¼" (6 mm) ball of green clay. Apply glue to the wire hook and insert it into the bottom of the boll. Shape the ball into an oval-like figure. Let it dry completely. This will become the center of the bud.

2"-2½" (5-6 cm)

2. Repeat step 4 of "Make the bract" to wrap clay around the stem. The clay should cover 2"-2½" (5-6 cm) of the wire. Let the stem dry completely.

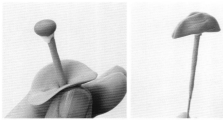

3. Make an unfurled leaf for the bud. Roll a ⅜" (1 cm) ball of green clay between your palms and shape it into a 1" (2.5 cm) -long teardrop. Place the clay on the pressing mat and flatten it with the pressing plate until it is 1" (2.5 cm) wide. Draw lines along the center and both sides of the back side with the rolling cutter. Insert the stem through the center. Apply glue to the base of the bud center to secure it. Fold the leaf in half to cover the bud center. Let the bud dry completely.

4. Make the leaves

Wrap the No. 24 wire with narrow floral tape and cut into quarters. Make seven.

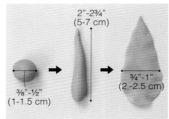

2"-2¾" (5-7 cm)

⅜"-½" (1-1.5 cm)

¾"-1" (2 -2.5 cm)

1. Roll a ⅜"-1/2" (1-1.5 cm) ball of green clay between your palms and shape it into a 2"-2¾" (5-7 cm) -long teardrop. Place the clay on the pressing mat and flatten it with the pressing plate until it is ¾"-1" (2 -2.5 cm) wide. Roll the modeling tool around the edges to add texture.

2. Lay the leaf in your palm with the top side of the leaf facing up. (The top side has visible fingerprints.) Draw a line along the center of the leaf and three lines on each side of the center vein with the rolling cutter.

3. Apply glue to the wire tip and lay it along the leaf's center vein. Pinch the leaf from the back side to secure the leaf. Make seven total, in both medium and large sizes.

5. Make the leaf without a stem *(for open flower and bud)*

1. Make a leaf for the open flower. Roll a ⅜" (1 cm) ball of green clay between your palms and shape it into a 1¾" (4.5 cm) -long teardrop. Place the clay on the pressing mat and flatten it with the pressing plate until it is 1" (2.5 cm) wide. Add slight texture to the edges with a modeling tool. On the top side of leaf, draw a line along the center and two lines on each side with with the rolling cutter. Fold in half to add dimension. Make two. Let them dry partially.

2. Apply glue to the base of the leaf and place it just below the flower to wrap the flower base. Place the second leaf on the opposite side of the stem, ½" (1.5 cm) below.

3. Make two more leaves in the same size as the one in step 3 of "Make the bud" and let them dry partially. Apply glue to the base of each leaf. Place the each leaf on the stem, facing each other. Insert the flower into the foam block to let dry completely.

6. Paint the flower

Place a small amount of each color needed on a plastic-wrapped paint palette or work surface. For the open flower, mix a base coat of blue and white, and paint it on, brushing from outside to the inside. Paint the tips and edges with purple mixed with blue to add detail. Paint white at the center of the petal, and paint the rest of the petal grass green. Paint the bract white.
For the leaf, mix a base coat from green and sage green. Paint a white line along the center leaf vein. Mix purple and brown and paint the base and tip of each leaf. Repeat for the leaves without wire stems.

7. Assemble the flower

Wrap the flower and bud stems with floral tape and secure the bigger leaves in place, facing each other. Attach all other stems and leaves to the main flower stem as shown in the photo.

SUMMER

Chinese Lantern

MATERIALS (for one branch)

Resin clay:
Fruit, fruit center: 2" (5 cm) ball
Flower: ⅝" (1.75 cm) ball
Calyx, leaf: 1⅝" (4 cm) ball
Leaf mold: 1¼" (3 cm) ball

Floral wire:
No. 26 2: flower stem, leaf
No. 24 3: leaf stem
No. 18 2: fruit stem, assembly

Floral tape: Light green (narrow and regular width)

Oil paint: green, dark green, grass green, pink, bright yellow, empire red, white, blue, yellow

Small pips—5 (flower center)

Prepare the clay

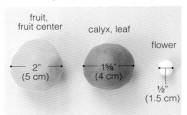

Prepare the clay. For the fruit and fruit center, add empire red and bright yellow to a 2" (5 cm) ball of white clay to make pale orange.

For the calyx and leaf, add green and dark green to a 1⅝" (4 cm) ball of clay to make green.

For the flower, add white to a ½" (1.5 cm) ball of white clay to make it more opaque.

1. Make an embossing leaf mold

See page 87 for a full-size fruit template. Trace shape onto tracing paper and use as a cutting guide when making the fruit.

Roll a 1¼" (3 cm) ball of clay into a 2⅜" (5.75 cm) -long teardrop. Place the clay on the pressing mat and flatten it until it is 1¾" (4.5 cm) wide. Lay it on the strawberry leaf mold to imprint it with the leaf vein. Let it dry completely. It will be used as a mold for embossing veins on the fruit.

2. Make the flower

Wrap the No. 26 wire with narrow tape and cut it into five equal pieces. Make a hook in one end of two of the pieces.
Paint the tips of the flower pips yellow and let dry.

1. Apply glue ⅜" (1 cm) below the tips of five flower pips. Let the glue dry partially and cut them in half. Apply glue to the bottom of the pips and attach them to the hook in the wire. Wrap the pips and entire wire two to three times with the narrow floral tape. Make two. This becomes the flower center.

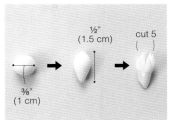

2. Make the flower. Roll a ⅜" (1 cm) ball of white clay and shape it into a ½" (1.5 cm) -long teardrop. Make five equal cuts in the thicker end of the clay. Spread the five pieces apart with the modeling tool, and make a line at the center of the petals. Pinch the tips of petals to shape them.

3. Insert the wire from step 1 through the center of the flower. Apply glue to the bottom of the flower center and secure it in place.

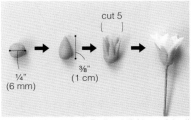

4. Make the calyx. Roll a ¼" (6 mm) ball of green clay and shape it into a ⅜" (1 cm) -long teardrop. Make five equal cuts in the thinner side of the clay. Spread each piece apart with the modeling tool. Insert the wire stem from the previous step and apply glue to the bottom of the flower to secure the calyx. Make one more. Insert the flower into the foam block to dry.

3. Make the fruit

You should make the fruit center ahead of time so it is completely dry before making the finished fruit.

1. Wrap the No. 18 wire with narrow floral tape and cut into four equal pieces. Make a hook in one end of three of the pieces. Roll a ⅝" (1.75 cm) ball of pale orange clay between your palms. Apply glue to the hook of the wire and insert the hook into the bottom center of the ball. Make three fruit centers. Let them dry completely.

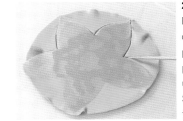

2. Begin shaping the fruit. Roll a 1" (2.5 cm) ball of pale orange clay between your palms. Place the clay on the pressing mat and flatten it until it is 4⅜" (11 cm) wide. Stretch the edges with your fingers to make them thinner. Place the template (from page 87) on the clay and trace the pattern with a bamboo stick. Again, stretch the edges to make them thinner.

3. Apply a small amount of hand cream to the leaf mold (for easy release). Place the mold against each petal-like section of the fruit to imprint the leaf veins on the clay.

4. Roll a ⅜" (1 cm) ball of pale orange clay and press it flat. Glue it to the middle of the clay shape. This becomes the base.

5. Insert the stem wire from step 1 through the fruit base. Apply glue to the bottom of the fruit center and on top of the base and secure them.

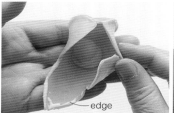

6. Apply a small line of glue along the edges of the fruit. Pinch each corner so they are secured in place.

7. Trim and reshape the edges of the fruit so they are rounded to finish. Make three. Let them dry completely.

4. Make the leaves

Wrap both the No. 26 and No. 24 wire with narrow floral tape. Cut the No. 26 into six equal pieces (two are for the small leaves). Cut the No. 24 into four equal pieces (ten are for the medium and large leaves).

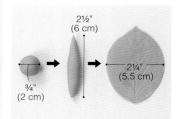

1. Roll a ¾" (2 cm) ball of green clay between your palms and shape it into a 2½" (6 cm) -long teardrop. Place the clay on the pressing mat and flatten it until it is 2¼" (5.5 cm) wide. Make an imprint of the leaf veins with the strawberry leaf mold.

2. Cut small V shapes into the edge of the leaf. Turn it over and add frilled texture to the edges with the modeling tool.

3. Apply glue to the tip of wire and lay it down along the leaf center. Pinch the leaf from behind to secure it. Make two small leaves, five medium leaves, and four large leaves. Let them dry completely.

5. Painting the flower and leaves

Place a small amount of each color on a plastic-wrapped paint palette or work surface.

1. Paint a white base coat on the flower, and add a touch of grass green towards the inside. Paint a green base coat on the leaf. Mix dark green with a bit of blue and paint details on the flower center.

2. Paint the fruit. Mix and paint a base coat of grass green and white for the top fruit. From the bottom, paint with empire red mixed with bright yellow. Add empire red details. Paint the fruit tip with green mixed with grass green. For the middle fruit, mix and paint a base coat of empire red and bright yellow. Paint the base of the fruit with empire red mixed with bright yellow. Add empire red details. Paint the tip green. Paint the bottom fruit with a base coat of empire red. Add empire red and pink details and shading, and pain the tip green.

Assembly notes
Attach the small leaves, facing each other, and the top of the branch, made from No. 18 wire. Below them, attach the medium leaves in the same manner, then attach the large leaves below them. Attach the fruit between the pairs of medium and large leaves.

SUMMER

Thistle

Prepare the clay

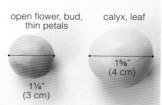

open flower, bud, thin petals   calyx, leaf

1⅝"
(4 cm)

1¼"
(3 cm)

For the open flower, bud, and thin petals, add peony and blue to 1¼" (3 cm) ball of white clay to make rose-colored clay.

For the calyx and leaf, add green and dark green to a 1⅝" (4 cm) ball of clay to make grass green.

MATERIALS (for 1 branch)

Resin clay:
Open flower, bud, thin petals: 1¼" (3 cm) ball
Calyx, leaf: 1⅝" (4 cm) ball

Floral wire:
No. 26   1 (small leaf stem)
No. 24   2 (medium/large leaf stem)
No. 18   1 (bud stem)
No. 16   2 (flower stem)

Floral tape: Light green (narrow and regular width)

Oil paint: peony, blue, green, dark green, white, pink, purple

Rose pips: 5 (flower center)

1. Make the open flower and bud

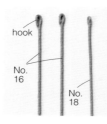

hook

No. 16

No. 18

1. Wrap one No. 18 (bud) and two No.16 wires (open flower) with regular width floral tape. Make a hook at one end of one piece.

¾"
(2 cm)

2. Make the thin petals of the open flower. Roll a ⅛" (3 mm) rose-colored ball of clay between your palms and shape it into a ¾" (2 cm) -long rice shape. Make fifty. Let the petals dry until they are hard.

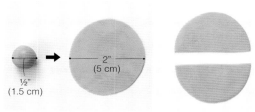

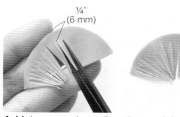

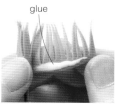

3. Make the open flower. Roll a ½" (1.5 cm) rose-colored ball of clay between your palms. Place the clay on the pressing mat and flatten it until it is 2" (5 cm) wide. Place it on the foam block until it is halfway dry. Cut it in half.

4. Make several cuts into the semicircle, from the middle toward the edge, creating a fringe. Leave a ¼" (6 mm) edge. Repeat on the other half.

5. With the fringe facing up, apply glue along the bottom edge. Start at the left side and affix one No. 16 hook along the edge. Wrap the clay around the hook, keeping it centered and level.

6. Pinch the base and spread the tips of the petals. This will become the flower center. Make a second flower center and let both dry completely.

7. Repeat steps 3-4: glue the rounded edge and wrap it around the flower center. Pinch the base to secure the clay and spread the tips of the petals.

8. Make one more row of petal-fringe and wrap it around the flower center and pinch against the base of the clay. Spread the tips of the petals and let the flower dry completely.

9. Apply glue to the tips of the petals made in step 2 and insert them in between flower center's petals to fill out the flower. Insert about twenty-five to create a full flower shape. Make two open flowers.

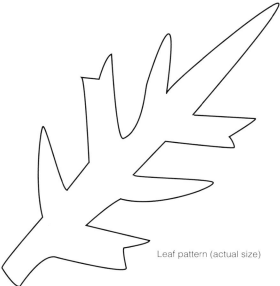

Leaf pattern (actual size)

Make the open flower and bud *(continued)*

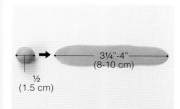

10. Make the bud. Roll a ½" (1.5 cm) ball of rose clay between your hands and and press it into a 3¼"-4" (8-10 cm) -long strip.

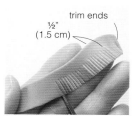

trim ends
½"
(1.5 cm)

11. Stretch the top edge to make it thinner. Make a cut every ⅛" (3 mm) the full length of the strip. Trim both ends so they are squared.

12. Apply glue to the hook of a No. 18 wire and affix to one edge of the fringed strip from step 11. Wrap the clay around the hook. Pinch the base to secure the clay. Let the bud dry completely.

2. Make the calyx

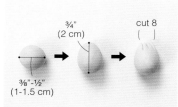

¾"
(2 cm)

cut 8
( )

⅜"-½"
(1-1.5 cm)

1. Roll two balls of grass-green clay between your palms: ⅜" (1 cm) for the bud and ⅝" (1.5 cm) for the open flower. Shape each ball into a ¾" (2 cm) -long teardrop. Make eight shallow cuts in the narrower end.

2. Insert the wide end of the modeling tool into the clay to create a wide, round hole (see page 107, Lily of the Valley, for more detailed instructions).

3. Insert the wire of the open flower stem into the middle of the calyx. Apply glue inside the calyx to secure it. Trim extra clay from the base of the calyx to round the bottom.

4. Turn the flower over and make small cuts into the clay from the bottom of the calyx toward the top. Repeat on each bud's calyx.

3. Make the leaves

Cut a No. 26 wire into six equal pieces for the small leaf. Cut a No. 24 wire into five equal pieces: three for medium leaves and two for large leaves. Trace the leaf pattern onto pattern paper.

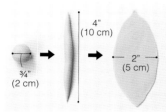

1. Make the large leaf. Roll a ¾" (2 cm) ball of grass-green clay into a 4" (10 cm) -long tube (with pointed ends). Place the clay on the pressing mat and flatten it until it is 2" (5 cm) wide.

2. Apply some hand cream to the back of the leaf pattern paper and onto a bamboo stick. Lay the pattern over the pressed clay and cut out the clay with the bamboo stick.

3. Roll the modeling tool across the back side of the leaf to thin the edges. Turn it over. Draw one line up the center of the leaf and each tooth with the rolling cutter.

4. Apply glue to half of the No. 24 wire and attach it to the leaf about 1" (3 cm) from the top. Pinch the leaf from the back to secure the clay to the wire. Modify the pattern shape for the small- and medium-sized leaves. Let the leaves dry completely.

4. Paint and assemble the flowers

Place a small amount of each color needed on a plastic-wrapped paint palette or work surface.

1. Mix a base coat of pink and purple for the flower. Paint the inside of the flower with peony mixed with blue. Paint the tips of the petals white.

2. Mix a base coat of green and mixed green, plus a bit of white, for the calyx. Paint the calyx with green mixed with dark green, brushing from bottom to top. Paint the edges of the calyx white. Repeat for the bud.

3. Mix a base coat of green and dark green for the leaves. Paint blue mixed with green from middle to the base. Paint a white line detail up the center.

4. Assemble the branch. Wrap a length of wire with one layer of narrow tape, then wrap it with regular width tape to thicken the stem. Attach a small leaf to the wire below the calyx. Place a medium leaf 2¾" (7 cm) below that. Place a large leaf 2" (5 cm) below it. Place the base of the bud stem slightly lower than the open flower and secure with regular width tape. Place another open flower just below it. Attach the large leaves at the base, facing each other. Wrap the stem with two layers of narrow tape to secure all pieces completely.

$\mathcal{A}$UTUMN

Bush Clover

MATERIALS (for 1 branch)

Resin clay:
Bud, flower center, outer petal: 1¼" (3 cm) ball
Inner petal: ¾" (2 cm) ball
Small bud: ¾" (2 cm) ball
Calyx, leaf: 1⅝" (4 cm) ball

Floral wire:
No. 28   10: bud and leaf stems
No. 26   5: open flower and leaf stems
No. 18   2 and No. 16   1 (for assembling the flower)

Floral tape: Light green (narrow and regular width)

Oil paint: green, dark green, grass green, sage green, blue, purple, pink, white

Prepare the clay

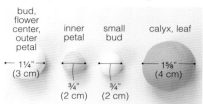

For the bud, flower center, and outer petal, add a very small amount of pink and purple to the 1 ¼" (3 cm) ball of clay to make light pink.

For the inner petal, add a lot more of pink and purple to the ¾" (2 cm) ball of clay to make dark pink.

For the small bud, add a touch of green to ¾" (2 cm) ball of clay to make light green.

For the calyx and leaf, add green and dark green to a 1⅝" (4 cm) ball of clay to make light green.

1. Make the open flower

Cut the No. 26 wire into six pieces. Make a hook at one end of each piece. Make thirty.

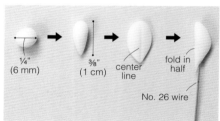

1. Make the flower center. Roll a ¼" (6 mm) ball of light pink clay into a ⅜" (1 cm) -long teardrop. Press the clay lightly with your finger to flatten it and press a line in the center of the clay teardrop with a modeling tool. Apply glue to the hook of a wire, lay it along the line and fold the clay in half around the wire.

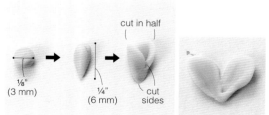

2. Make the inner petal. Roll a ⅛" (3 mm) ball of dark pink clay into ¼" (6 mm) -long teardrop. Cut in half at the thicker end of the teardrop and spread apart with the modeling tool. Make small cuts at the sides as shown.

3. Apply glue to the bottom of the inner petal and glue in place so it covers the flower center.

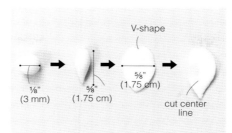

V-shape

⅛"
(3 mm)

⅝"
(1.75 cm)

⅝"
(1.75 cm)

cut center line

4. Make the outer petal. Roll an ⅛" (3 mm) ball of light pink clay into a ⅝" (1.75 cm) -long teardrop. Press it with your fingers until it is ⅝" (1.75 cm) wide. Cut a small V shape at the top of the petal. Use the mod-eling tool to add a curl to the edge. Press a line in the center. Fold the petal in half and curl the top edge outwards.

5. Apply glue to the inside base of the outer petal and attach it to the base of the inner petal. Stretch the upper part of the outer petal outwards a bit more.

2. Make the calyx

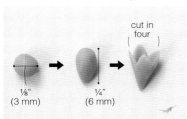

cut in four

⅛"
(3 mm)

¼"
(6 mm)

1. Roll a ⅛" (3 mm) ball of light green clay into a ¼" (6 mm) -long, fat teardrop. Make four small cuts in the thicker end and spread each tip apart with the modeling tool.

2. Insert the open flower wire stem through the center of the calyx. Apply glue at the base of the outer petals to secure the calyx. Align one petal of the calyx at the center front. Make thirty. Let them dry completely.

3. Make the bud

* Cut No. 28 wire into six equal pieces and make a hook at one end of each piece. Make thirty.

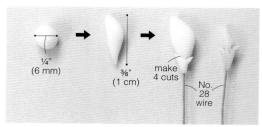

¼"
(6 mm)

⅜"
(1 cm)

make
4 cuts

No.
28
wire

Roll a ¼" (6 mm) ball of light pink clay into a ⅜" (1 cm) -long teardrop. Then reshape the wide end into a paddle-like shape. Apply glue to the tip of the hook and insert it into the bottom of the clay. Cut the bottom of the clay into four pieces to make the calyx. For the small bud, repeat this step with a smaller amount of light green clay. Make thirty total. Let them dry completely.

4. Make the leaves

* Cut No. 28 wire into six equal pieces. Make thirty.

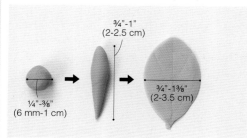

¾"-1"
(2-2.5 cm)

¼"-⅜"
(6 mm-1 cm)

¾"-1⅜"
(2-3.5 cm)

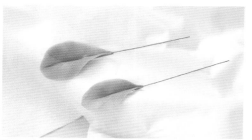

1. Roll two sizes of light green clay balls: 1/4" (6 mm) for small leaves and 3/8" (1 cm) for large leaves. Shape each ball into a ¾" (2 cm) -long (small) or a 1⅜" (3.5 cm) -long (large) teardrop. Place the clay on the pressing mat and flatten it with the pressing plate until it is either ¾" (2 cm) or 1" (2.5 cm) wide. Stretch the edges with your fingers to make them thinner. Lay it on the strawberry leaf mold to lightly imprint the leaf veins.

2. Apply glue to the tip of the wire and lay it along the center leaf vein. Pinch the leaf from behind to secure the wire to the leaf. Make thirty total, both small and large. Let the leaves dry completely.

3. Paint the flower

*Place a small amount of each color on a plastic-wrapped paint palette or work surface.

1. Mix a base coat of pink and white for the outer petal of the open flower. Mix a base coat of pink and purple for the inner petal. Paint details on the inner petals with pink mixed with purple. Paint the insides of the flower with pink mixed with purple. Lightly paint the tip of the flower center with grass green. Paint the calyx with sage green mixed with green.

2. Mix a base coat for the bud of pink and white. Paint the bud center with pink mixed with purple. Paint the tip grass green. For the calyx, follow the instructions for the open flower.

3. Mix a base coat for the small bud of green and white. For the calyx, follow the instructions for the open flower.

4. Make a three-leaf cluster. The large leaf is the center. Place the small leaves 2" (5 cm) below the large leaf and wrap with narrow tape. Make ten. Paint the leaves. Mix a base coat of green and dark green. Paint the center part with blue mixed with green. Draw a white line at the center of each leaf, brushing from bottom to top.

6. Assemble the flower

As shown at left, gather the flowers and leaves into a small bundle. Wrap a No. 18 wire with regular width floral tape to start the branch. Wrap all stems to secure them to the branch. Small branches can be made by gathering two stems with No. 16 wire and wrapping with floral tape.

Chinese Lantern
(actual size), page 76

Αutumn

Balloon Flower

MATERIALS

Resin clay:
Pistil, stamen: ⅜" (1 cm) ball
Ovary, bud: ¾" (2 cm) ball
Flower, half-open flower: 1¼" (3 cm) ball
Calyx, leaf: 1⅜" (3.5 cm) ball

Floral wire:
No. 26 1: small leaf stem
No. 24 2: medium and large leaf stem
No. 18 1: bud stem
No. 16 2: flower and half-open flower stem

Floral tape: Light green (narrow and regular width)

Oil paint: green, dark green, grass green, blue, purple, white

Prepare the clay

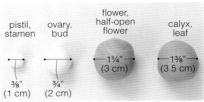

For the pistil and stamen, add a small amount of white to a ⅜" (1 cm) ball of clay to make white.

For the ovary and bud, add green to a ¾" (2 cm) ball to make light green

For the flower and half-open flower, add purple and blue to a 1¼" (3 cm) ball of clay to make bluish purple.

For the calyx and leaf, add green and dark green to a 1⅜" (3.5 cm) ball of clay to make dark green.

1. Make the flower center

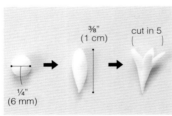

1. Make the pistil. Roll a ¼" (6 mm) ball of white clay into a 3/8" (1 cm) -long teardrop. Make five cuts into the thick end of the teardrop and spread each piece apart with a thin modeling tool. Let dry completely.

2. Make the stamen. Roll a ⅛" (3 mm) ball of white clay into a ½" (1.5 cm) -long tube. Bend them into L shapes (with the shorter leg at the bottom). Make five. Let them dry completely.

3. Wrap the No. 16 wire with regular floral tape and make a hook at one end. Make the ovary: roll a ⅜" (1 cm) ball of light green clay into a ⅜" (1 cm) -long teardrop. Apply glue to the hook of the wire and insert into the bottom of the clay teardrop.

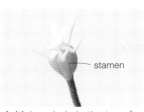

stamen

4. Make a hole in the top of the ovary. Apply glue to the bottom of the pistil and insert it into the hole. Draw (imprint) five vertical lines around the ovary. Apply glue where the stamen will be attached, then attach the five stamen around the pistil. Insert flower center in the foam block and let dry completely.

ovary

pistil

5. Make for a second (open) flower center. Follow steps 1-4 to make the stamen, ovary, and pistil. Assemble, then let dry completely.

2. Make the bud

For the stem, wrap the No. 18 wire with regular floral tape and make a hook in one end.

1. Roll a ¾" (2 cm) ball into a 1" (2.5 cm) -long teardrop. Press the modeling tool into all four sides to make four indentations.

2. Apply glue to the hook of the wire and insert it into the bottom of the clay teardrop. Pinch the clay to secure it to the wire. Draw five lines with the blade of the scissors at the base of the five raised sections of the bud. Let dry completely.

3. Make the open flower

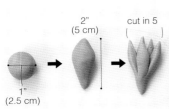

2"
(5 cm)

cut in 5

1"
(2.5 cm)

1. Roll a 1" (2.5 cm) ball of bluish-purple clay into a 2" (5 cm) -long teardrop with pointed ends. Make five deep cuts into the top of the clay.

2. Roll the thicker end of a modeling tool against each piece to spread it into a 1" (2.5 cm) -wide petal. Each petal should be the same width.

3. Roll the thinner end of the modeling tool against the petals to make them thinner.

4. Cut between the petals with scissors to separate them.

5. Gently etch lines in the petals with the blade of the scissors. Make one line at the center and small lines at the edges of the petals.

6. Pinch the tip of the petals so they come to a sharp point. Insert the wire of the flower center through the top. Apply glue to the inside base of the flower to secure to the wire. Make the half-open flower slightly smaller and bend the petals inward. Let both dry completely.

4. Make the calyx

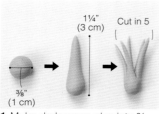

1¼" (3 cm)   Cut in 5

⅜" (1 cm)

1. Make dark green clay into ⅜ inch ball, then shape it to 1⅛ inch long tear drop shape. Cut in 5 from thinner side and spread each 5 pieces with the tool.

2. Insert the wire of open flower to calyx. Apply glue to the bottom of the open flower and stick them. Note to place each pieces of calyx in between the flower petals.

3. Press the tool at the bottom of each pieces of calyx to make dents. Do the same to all pieces. Follow same procedure for the half open flower to apply calyx. Dry both 2 pieces (open flower and half open)

5. Make the leaves

For the stem wire, cut the No. 26 wire into six equal pieces and use five (for the small leaves).
Cut the No. 24 wire into four equal pieces and make six (for the medium/large leaves).

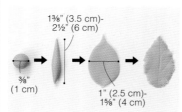

1⅜" (3.5 cm)-2½" (6 cm)

⅜" (1 cm)

1" (2.5 cm)-1⅝" (4 cm)

1. Roll two sizes of dark green clay balls: ⅜" (1 cm) (small) and ¾" (2 cm) (large). Shape the small ball into a 1⅜" (3.5 cm) -long teardrop and the large ball into a 2½" (6 cm) -long teardrop. Press the clay flat: the small shape is 1" (2.5 cm) wide and the large shape is 1⅝" (4 cm) wide. Stretch the edges with your finger to make it thinner. Press the clay onto the strawberry leaf mold to make an imprint of the leaf vein. From the back side, roll the modeling tool along the edges to add frills and tex-ture. Finish the leaf edges with a zigzag shape. (For complete instructions, see Cyclamen, page 51.)

small   medium   large

2. Apply glue to the top of the wire and attach it to the center leaf vein. Pinch the leaf from behind to secure the wire to the leaf. Make five small, two medium, and four large leaves. Let the leaves dry completely.

6. Paint the flowers and leaves

Place a small amount of each color on a plastic-wrapped paint palette or work surface.

For the flowers: Mix a base coat of purple and a small amount of blue for the petals. Paint white at the base of the petals, and grass green on the ovary. Detail the edges of the petals with purple mixed with blue. Paint a green base coat on the calyx. Paint the calyx edges white and the base dark green.

For the bud: Mix a mint-green base coat (green and white). Paint the lower half of the flower grass green to darken it. Paint purple and blue details at the top. For bud's calyx, follow the same instructions as for the flowers.

For the leaf: Pain a green base coat. Paint the leaf centers dark green. Draw a white line down the center of each leaf at the center leaf vein.

To assemble:
Wrap two small leaves against the stem of the half-open flower and bud with tape, and tape one to the open flower. Gather together the flower and half-open flower and attach one medium leaf with tape. Tape the bud below that one, and tape additional medium/large leaves in a spiral down the stem.

Summer

Lily

Prepare the clay

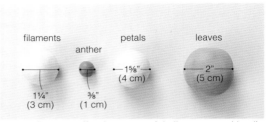

filaments | petals | leaves
anther

1¼" (3 cm) | ⅜" (1 cm) | 1⅝" (4 cm) | 2" (5 cm)

For the filaments (for the stamen/pistil, ovary, and bud), add a small amount of green to a 1¼" (3 cm) ball of clay to make mint green.

For the anther (on the stamen), add brown to a ⅜" (1 cm) ball of white clay to make brown.

For the inner and outer petals, add pink to 1⅝" (4 cm) ball of clay to make pale pink.

For the leaves, add green and dark green to a 2" (5 cm) ball of clay to make green.

MATERIALS (for 1 branch)

Resin clay:
Stalks (for stamen/pistil, ovary, bud): 1¼" (3 cm) ball
Anther (for stamen) ⅜" (1 cm) ball
Inner/outer petal: 1⅝" (4 cm)
Leaf: 2" (5 cm)

Floral wire:
No. 26 9: stem for pistil/stamen, flower, leaf
No. 24 3: leaf stem
No. 18 3: bud, center of ovary stem

Floral tape: Light green (narrow and regular width)

Oil paint: green, dark green, blue, purple, pink, yellow, brown, dark brown, white

Corn starch (pollen; see "Attach the anthers" in step 2)

1. Make pistil and stamen

Cut the No. 26 wire into four equal pieces. Prepare seven of them.

1. Make the pistil. Roll a ¼" (6 mm) mint green ball of clay into a 1¼" (3 cm) -long tube. Press a bamboo stick along the center of the tube to make a slight indent in the clay.

2. Apply glue along the center of a 2⅜" (5.75 cm) -long wire and lay it within the dent. Wrap the clay around the wire.

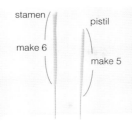

3. Roll the wire and clay on the tabletop until the clay covers the one end of the wire. The clay should overhang about ¼" (6 mm).

4. Press the bamboo stick into the end of the clay tube tip to make three small indents.

stamen

make 6

pistil

make 5

5. Make the stamen. Roll a ¼" (6 mm) ball of mint green clay into a long string and attach to the wire in the same manner as for the pistil (above). Roll it on the tabletop until it is 2" (5 cm) long. Make six. Let the stamen and pistils dry completely. Follow the same steps for the pistil and stamen for the half-open flower.

2. Attach the anthers

press

1. Roll a ¼" (6 mm) ball of brown clay into a ⅜" (1 cm) -long string. Poke a small hole with the tip of the bamboo stick into the end.

2. Apply glue to the tip of the stamen and insert it into the hole made in step 1. Gently press a scissor blade to the upper part of the anther to make a line. Make six. Let them dry completely.

3. Make the pollen. Mix a small amount of brown and dark brown oil paint with the cornstarch. Mix well with a paintbrush. Paint the anthers with heavy coat of brown paint. While it is still wet, attach the pollen. Make six and let them dry. Follow the same steps for the pistil and stamen for the half-open flower.

3. Make the petals

Prepare wire for the stems. Cut a strip of regular-width floral tape in thirds. Wrap the tape tightly around the No. 26 wire. Cut in four. Prepare twelve for the open flower and half-open flower.

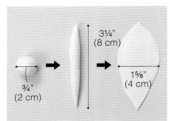

1. Make the inner petals. Roll a ¾" (2 cm) ball of pale pink clay into a 3¼" (8 cm) -long tube. Place the clay on the pressing mat and flatten it until it is 1⅝" (4 cm) wide. Stretch the edge with your finger to make it thinner.

2. Roll the modeling tool around the edges of the petal to add a lot of frills and texture. Turn the petal over. Fold the sides of the petal inward slightly to make the petals tent-shaped.

3. Gently make a line on the top center with the rolling cutter. Make an additional four lines at each of the sides.

4. Apply glue to the wire and attach it one-third of the way up the petal. Pinch from behind to hide the wire. Sharpen the ends of the petal by pinching them with your fingers. Make three.

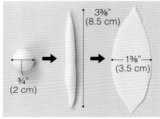

5. Make the outer petals. Roll a ¾" (2 cm) ball of pale pink clay into a 3⅜" (8.5 cm) -long tube. Place the clay on the pressing mat and flatten it until it is 1⅜" (3.5 cm) wide. Stretch the edge with your finger to make it thinner.

6. Roll the modeling tool around the edges of the petal to add a lot of frills and texture. Turn the petal over. Press the petal center with the modeling tool to make an indent.

7. Draw a line along the petal center with the rolling cutter. Make an additional four or five lines at the sides. Attach a wire for a stem as in step 4. Pinch the tip of the petal. Make three.

8. Place tissue paper on top of the foam block. Arrange the inner and outer petals to dry on the block so the tips of the petals overhang the edges. Let the petals dry completely.

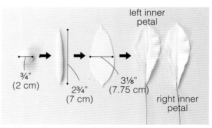

9. Make the petals for the half-open flower. Instructions are given for the inner petals, and the outer petal instructions are in parentheses. Roll a ¾" (2 cm) ball of pale pink clay into a 2¾" (7 cm) (3⅛" [7.75 cm]) -long string shape. Place the clay on the pressing mat and flatten it until it is 1¼" (3 cm) wide. Stretch the edge with your finger to make it thinner. Shape as for the open flower and attach wire. Make three of each size, and let the petals dry completely.

4. Make the bud

Wrap the No.18 wire with narrow tape and cut in two. Make a hook in one end. Make one.

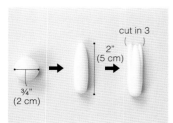

1. Roll a ¾" (2 cm) ball of mint green clay into a 2" (5 cm) -long teardrop. Make three cuts into the clay at the thin end.

2. Pinch the cut clay closed again. Apply glue to the wire hook and insert it into the bottom of the clay. Imprint lines down the length of the clay with a scissor blade, starting at the cuts made in step 1.

3. Press deeper lines between (at the midpoint) each of the three cuts with a scissor blade. Press a few smaller lines around it. Insert the stem into the foam block to dry completely.

5. Make the leaves

Prepare the wires for the stems. Wrap No. 26 and No. 24 wires with a strip of regular width floral tape cut in thirds. Cut the No. 26 wire into six equal pieces for the small leaf, and make eight of them. Cut the No. 24 into four equal pieces for the medium/large leaf, and make ten.

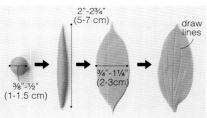

1. Roll a ⅜"-1/2" (1-1.5 cm) ball of green clay into a 2"-2¾" (5-7 cm) -long tube. Place the clay on the pressing mat and flatten it until it is 3/4"-1¼" (2-3 cm) wide. Stretch the edge with your finger to make it thinner. Gently draw a line up the leaf center and two more on both sides of the center line with your rolling cutter.

2. Apply glue to the wire and affix it about halfway up the leaf. Pinch the leaf from behind to secure it. Bend the leap tip outwards slightly for added detail. Make eighteen total in small, medium, and large. Let the leaves dry completely.

6. Paint the flowers and leaves
Place a small amount of each color on a plastic-wrapped paint palette or work surface.

1. Mix a base coat of pink and white for the petals. Paint a light coat on the back of the petals. Paint the petal centers with pink mixed with purple. Mix purple and brown and paint spots on the lower parts of the petals.

2. Mix a base coat of green mixed with white for the bud. Paint the base and indented lines green. Paint a light coat of pink at the center for added detail. Paint the upper part dark brown. Paint a base coat of green on the leaf, adding a light coat on the back side. Mix green and blue, and apply the paint from the center to bottom.

7. Assemble the flower and leaves

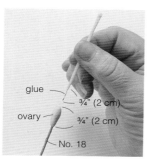

glue
¾" (2 cm)
ovary
¾" (2 cm)
No. 18

1. Make the ovary. Roll a ⅜" (1 cm) ball of mint green clay into a ¾" (2 cm) -long teardrop. Apply glue to the tip of the No. 18 wire (wrapped with regular-width tape) and insert it into the bottom of the clay. Cut the wire for the bottom of the pistil so it is ¾" (2 cm) long. Apply glue and insert the wire into the upper center of ovary to secure.

2. While the ovary is still pliable, gather six stamens around it evenly and secure them in place. Wrap the stems with narrow tape and wrap it all the way down to the base of the wire. Hold the middle filament and bend the stamens outward.

3. Paint the tip of pistil brown. Place three inner petals around the ovary, wrap the bases with narrow tape. Align three outer petals between the inner petals. Wrap the bases two or three times with narrow tape.

4. Wrap the base of the flower again with regular width tape to make it thicker, leaving 2" (5 cm) of wire exposed at the bottom. Attach a small leaf to the wire and wrap the stem with regular width tape. Wrap a few times from the bottom of the leaf to about 4½"-5" (10.5-12.5 cm) below to thicken it. Burnish the stem with the side of the pliers to make it shiny. Make the half-open flower slightly smaller. Close the flower.

5. Wrap the bud's stem from the base to 2" (5 cm) below it with tissue paper first, then twice with regular width tape to thicken it. Burnish the stem with the side of the pliers to make it shiny. Attach a small leaf 2" (5 cm) below the bud and wrap the stem with regular width tape. Wrap the stem with tissue paper and regular-width tape to thicken it. Burnish the stem with the side of the pliers to make it shiny.

For tips on assembling the flowers and remaining leaves, see the gallery photo on page 16.

96

AMAZING CLAY FLOWERS

ꙎINTER

Narcissus

MATERIALS (for one branch)

Resin clay:
Bud, flower, half-open flower: 1" (2.5 cm) ball
Trumpet: ⅝" (1.75 cm) ball
Bract: ⅜" (1 cm) ball
Calyx, leaf: 1⅝" (4 cm) ball

Floral wire:
No. 22 3: stem for bud, flower, half-open flower, leaf
No. 18 1: assembling the flower

Floral tape:
Light green (narrow)

Oil paint: green, dark green, grass green, sage green, yellow, bright yellow, dark brown, white

Rose pips
6 (flower center)

Prepare the clay

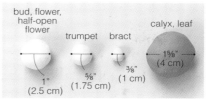

For the bud, flower, and half-open flower, add white to a 1" (2.5 cm) ball of clay to make white.
For the trumpet, add yellow to a ⅝" (1.75 cm) ball of clay to make yellow.
For the bract, add a bit of dark brown to a ⅜" (1 cm) ball of clay to make beige.
For the calyx and leaf, add green and dark green to a 1⅝" (4 cm) ball of clay to make green.

1. Make the flower, half-open flower, and bud

* Wrap the No. 22 wire with narrow floral tape. Cut in four equal pieces. Make a hook in one end of all four pieces.

* Paint the tips of the six rose pips yellow. Apply glue ⅜" (1 cm) below the tips. Cut the pips in two, below the glue. (See page 46 Cherry Blossom instructions.)

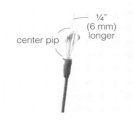

1. Make the flower center. Insert one center pip through the middle of the cluster of six pips and pull it through so it sits ¼" (6 mm) higher than the rest.. Apply glue to the hook of the wire, attach the pips to the hook, and wrap the base with narrow tape. Make two.

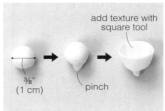

2. Make the trumpet. Pinch the base of a ⅜" (1 cm) ball of yellow clay to make one point. Spread the top of the ball into a cup shape with the modeling tool. Roll a square-shaped modeling tool along the inside to create texture.

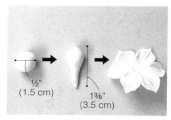

3. Press the tip of the square tool inward around the edge to make indentations. Insert the flower center from step 1 through the center. Apply glue to the base and pull the wire through the clay until the pistil/stamen is nested inside the trumpet. Make two. Let them dry completely.

4. Make the open flower. Roll a ½" (1.5 cm) ball of white clay into a 1⅜" (3.5 cm) -long rounded, elongated teardrop. Cut the rounded end in six equal pieces. Spread each piece apart with the modeling tool until they are each ¾" (2 cm) wide. Shape the petals so there is a slight peak at the center. Pinch the petal tips to shape them..

5. Cut between the petals to separate them. Layer the edges of one petal over, one under, and so on. Insert the trumpet through the flower center. Apply glue to the base and secure the trumpet.

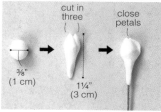

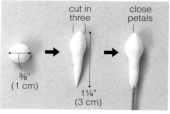

6. Make a slightly smaller version of the flower, following steps 4-5. This will be the small open flower. Close the petals slightly inward.

7. Make the half-open flower. Roll a ⅜" (1 cm) ball of white clay into a 1¼" (3 cm) -long, rounded, elongated teardrop. Cut the round end in three and spread each piece with the modeling tool, then close them again. The petals should be more tightly closed than the half-opened flower. Apply glue to the hook of the wire stem and insert it into the base of the clay.

8. Make the bud. Roll a ⅜" (1 cm) ball of white clay into a 1¼" (3 cm) -long, rounded, elongated teardrop. Cut the round end in three, then close them again. Apply glue to the hook of the wire stem and insert it into the base of the clay.

9. Make and attach the calyx. Roll a ¼" (6 mm) ball of green clay into a ⅜" (1 cm) -long teardrop. Make a hole in the thick end and insert a wire stem. Apply glue to the calyx to secure it to the flowers. Make three: flower, half-open flower, and bud.

2. Make the leaves

Wrap the No. 22 wire with narrow floral tape and cut it in three equal pieces. Prepare five of them. Roll a ¾" (2 cm) ball of green clay into a 7¼" (18.5 cm) -long tube. Press it flat with the pressing plate so it is ⅝" (1.75 cm) wide. Thin the edges and draw lines in the surface with the brush of a quilting pencil. Apply glue to the wire and lay it along half of the leaf. Make five. Let them dry completely.

3. Paint the flower

*Place a small amount of each color on a plastic-wrapped paint palette or work surface.

Paint a white base coat on the flower. Paint a light coat of green mixed with grass green at the inside of the flower. Paint the base of the flower green. Pain a base coat of yellow on the trumpet. Add bright yellow details here and there. Paint a white base coat on the half-open flower and bud. Paint the lower part of the half-open flower and bud with green mixed with sage green. Paint green mixed with dark green for the calyx. Paint a base coat of green mixed with sage green on the leaf. Add dark green details to the leaf.

4. Assemble the flower

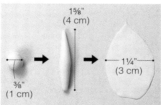

1⅝"
(4 cm)

⅜"
(1 cm)

1¼"
(3 cm)

99

NARCISSUS

1. For the flower and half-open flower and bud, wrap the stem with narrow floral tape starting at the bottom of the calyx. Gather the four stems, with the bud facing down, and tape them together. Arrange it at the top of the No. 18 wire (cut to two-thirds its length and wrapped tightly with floral tape) and wrap them together with tape. Wrap the stem with tissue paper and then with more layers of tape until the stem is ¼" (6 mm) thick. Burnish the stem with the side of the pliers to make it shiny.

2. Make the bract. Roll a ⅜" (1 cm) ball of beige clay into a 1⅝" (4 cm) -long teardrop. Press it with the presser plate until it is 1 1/4" (3 cm) wide. Roll the modeling tool along the edges to make it thinner and to add frills. Draw light lines in the bract with the rolling cutter. Apply glue to the bottom edge and attach it as though you are wrapping it around the bottom of the flowers with the pointed end at the top. Bend the tip of the bract outward.

3. Place five leaves around the stem about 8" (approx. 20 cm) below the bract and secure to the branch with tape. The flowers should face front and the leaves can fall outward.

Ⓦinter

Winter Aconite

MATERIALS (for seven open flowers, three half-open flowers, and three buds)

Resin clay:
Bud center, half-open flower, open-flower: 1¼" (3 cm) ball
Leaf: 1¼" (3 cm) ball
Leaf bud: ½" (1.5 cm)

Floral wire:
No. 28 8: leaf stems
No. 22 4: stems for flowers and bud

Floral tape: Mint green (narrow)

Faux flower stamens (or floral pips): 3 packages/bunches

Oil paint: dark green, sage green, grass green, yellow, purple, brown, dark brown, white

Extra-small flower pip—1 bunch (flower center)

Rose pip—1 bunch (flower center)

Prepare the clay

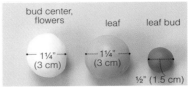

bud center, flowers   leaf   leaf bud

1¼" (3 cm)   1¼" (3 cm)   ½" (1.5 cm)

For the bud center and both flowers, add a small amount of white to a 1¼" (3 cm) ball of clay to make white
For the leaf, add dark green to a 1¼" (3 cm) ball of clay to make light green.
For the leaf bud, add a small amount of purple and dark brown to a ½" (1.5 cm) ball of clay to make purplish brown.

1. Make the bud

⅜" (1 cm)

1. Apply glue to the hook of the wire and insert it into a ¼" (6 mm) ball of white clay. Shape the ball into a ⅜" (1 cm) -long teardrop shape. This is the bud center.

2. Roll a purplish-brown ¼" (6 mm) ball of clay into a ⅜" (1 cm) -long teardrop. Cut the thinner end into twelve pieces. Spread each piece apart with the tool.

3. Insert the No. 22 wire through the center of the bud. Apply glue to the base of the bud center to secure the wire. Wrap the stem twice with tape. Make three of them. Let dry completely.

3. Make the open and half-open flowers

* Wrap the No. 22 wire with floral tape and cut in four equal pieces. Make a hook in one end. Prepare ten.

*Paint the tips of the extra-small pips with a mixed chocolate color (purple + brown). Paint the tip of the rose pips yellow. Let dry.

1. Apply glue ⅝" (1.75 cm) to the tips of thirty extra-small pips (which will be the stamen). Attach them to the top of the wire and insert the unpainted three pips (the pistil) ¼" (6 mm) so they stick out a bit further than the other pips.

2. Apply glue ⅜" (1 cm) to tips of sixteen rose pips. Trim the ends. Attach them around the stamen and wrap them with tape. This is the flower center.

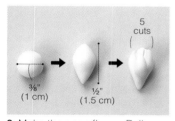

3. Make the open flower. Roll a ⅜" (1 cm) ball of white clay and shape it into a ½" (1.5 cm) -long fat tear-drop. Make five deep cuts in the wider end. Spread each piece with the modeling tool. Make an imprint at the center of the flower with the ball-end tool.

4. Press a rounded tool at the edges of the petals to draw lines in the clay.

5. Cut between the petals with scissors. Pinch the tips of the petals to shape them.

6. Insert the flower center from step 2 through the center of the petals. Apply glue to the base of the flower center to secure the center to the petals.

7. Make seven open flowers following the above steps.

8. Make three half-open flowers following the same instructions as for the open flower. Instead of keeping the petals open, close them halfway so they overlap each other.

3. Make the leaves
Cut the No. 28 wire into four equal pieces. Prepare thirty.

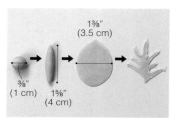

1. Roll a ⅜" (1 cm) ball of sage green clay into a 1⅝" (4 cm) -long string. Place the clay on the pressing mat and flatten it until it is 1⅜" (3.5 cm) wide. Cut out a leaf shape, using the full-size template shown below.

2. Lightly press a pointed modeling tool onto each leaf frond to make light indents.

3. Apply glue to the wire and lay it flat along the center of of the leaf and pinch it from behind to secure to the clay. Make thirty.

4. Paint and assemble the flower
Place a small amount of each color on a plastic-wrapped paint palette or work surface.

white dot

1. Paint a white base coat on the petals. Paint lightly the inside base of the petals with grass green.

2. For the bud, paint with purple mixed with a small amount of brown at the base. Paint the same color on the top of the stem.

3. Paint a base coat of sage green on the leaves. Paint the middle of each leaf dark green. Paint the base of the leaves white. Make four white dots at the center. Finally, mix purple and brown and add a light coat of this color over the white at the bottom of leaf.

4. Wrap the stem from the bottom of the flower to ⅜"-¾" (1-2 cm) below with floral tape to thicken it. Attach three leaves ⅜"-¾"" (1-2 cm) below the bottom of the leaf. Wrap with floral tape to secure leaves. Wrap a few more times to make stem thicker. Paint the stem with a light coat of purple mixed with brown.

Leaf template (actual size)

Autumn

Eulalia

MATERIALS (for one stalk)

Resin clay:
Ear: 1¼" (3 cm) ball
Leaf: 1¼" (3 cm) ball

Floral wire:
No. 22   14: stem
No. 14   1: assembly

Floral tape:
Light green (narrow and regular width)

Oil paint: brown, dark brown, green, dark green, grass green, sage green, blue, white

Hemp thread (for the ear)

Prepare the clay

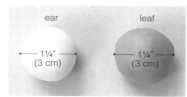

ear   leaf

1¼"   1¼"
(3 cm)   (3 cm)

For the ear, add a small amount of brown to a 1¼" (3 cm) ball of white clay to make beige. For the leaf, add green and dark green to a 1¼" (3 cm) ball of white clay to make green.

1. Make the ear

Cut the No. 22 wire into two equal pieces. Prepare twenty.

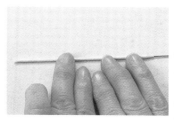

1. Roll a ⅜" (1 cm) ball of beige clay into a 2" (5 cm) -long, thin snake. Make a dent along the center line of the clay. Apply glue along about 5" (13 cm) of the wire and lay it down into the dent. Roll the clay and wire on the table until it is 4¾"-5" (12-12.5 cm) long. (See page 92, Lily, for full instructions on this technique.)

2. Snip a narrow V shape in the clay every ⅝" (1.75 cm).

3. Cut the hemp thread into ¾" (2 cm) lengths. Fray the threads, then bundle three or four fibers in a cluster. Apply glue to the bottom tips and insert them into a V shaped cut to secure them.

4. Make twenty of these and let them dry completely.

2. Make the leaves

For the small leaf, use one of the cut pieces. For the large leaf, use a full-length wire for each leaf.

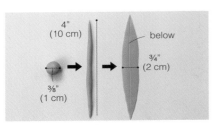

1. Make one small leaf. Roll a ⅜" (1 cm) ball of green clay into a 4" (10 cm) -long, thin snake. Place the clay on the pressing mat and flatten it until it is ¾" (2 cm) wide. Stretch the edge to make it thinner. Draw lines and texture on the leaf using the brush of a quilter's pencil. Draw a line down the leaf center with a rolling cutter. (See page xx, Lily of the Valley, for full instructions on this technique.)

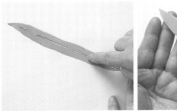 

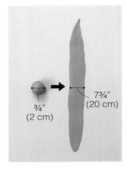

3. Make three large leaves. Roll a ¾" (2 cm) ball of green clay into a to 7¾" (20 cm) long snake. Place the clay on the pressing mat and flatten it until it is ¾" (2 cm) wide. Stretch the edge. Draw a line down the leaf center, repeating steps 1 and 2. Affix the wire and let it dry.

2. Apply glue along half the wire and attach it along the center line and affix the wire to the leaf. Let it dry completely.

3. Painting the ear and leaves

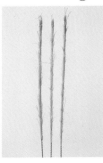

1. Paint the ear. Mix a base coat of white and dark brown to make a light beige. Paint a light coat of brown and dark brown on the upper part to add detail. Paint a light coat of grass green on the bottom part.

2. Mix a base coat of green and sage green for the leaf. Paint a light coat on the back of the leaf. Paint a few details on the front edges with green mixed with a touch of blue. Paint the edge with dark brown to highlight.

4. Assemble the stalk

Place a small amount of each color on a plastic-wrapped paint palette or work surface.

1. Wrap the No. 14 wire with narrow floral tape. Gather three ears and align the wire tips to the No. 14 wire. Wrap the wires together with narrow tape. Attach another three ears ⅜" (1 cm) below the first on the No. 14 wire and wrap those with tape. Again, attach another bundle ⅜" (1 cm) below the second. Repeat this until twenty ears have been attached. Wrap the stem several times with floral tape to make it thicker.

2. Attach a small leaf 2" (5 cm) below the ears and wrap the stem with regular width tape. Wrap the stem from the leaf to 5"-5½" (12.5-13.5 cm) below with tissue paper and regular width tape to make it thicker. Attach three large leaves along the thick stem, positioning each one lower than the previous one, and wrapping each with regular width tape. The stem can be made even thicker by wrapping it with a layer of tissue paper and binding it with a layer of regular width tape.

⒜UTUMN

Stonecrop

MATERIALS (for two branches)

Resin clay:
Flower center, flower: ⅝" (1.75 cm) ball
Bud, leaf: 1⅝" (4 cm) ball

Floral wire:
No. 28 6: bud and flower stem
No. 26 3: leaf stem
No. 18 2: assembly

Floral tape:
Light green (narrow and regular width)

Oil paint: green, dark green, sage green, purple, pink, peony, brown white

Extra-small pips—40

Prepare the clay

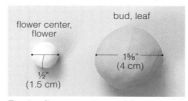

For the flower center and flower, add pink to a ½" (1.5 cm) ball of white clay to make pink.
For the bud and leaf, add green and sage green to a 1⅝" (4 cm) ball of white clay to make light green.

1. Make the flower and bud

Cut the No. 28 wire into six and make a hook in one end of each. Prepare fifteen for the flower center and eighteen for the bud.

1. Make the flower center. Roll a ⅛" (3 mm) ball of pink clay into a fat teardrop. Apply glue to the hook of the wire and insert it into the bottom of the clay. Make five small cuts in the top of the teardrop.

2. Paint the ends of the extra-small pips pink and cut them into ⅜" (1 cm) lengths. Apply glue around the flower center (from step 1) and attach five pips, one by one.

Make the flower and bud (continued)

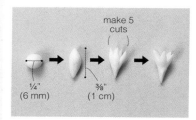

3. Make the flower. Roll a ¼" (6 mm) ball of pink clay into a 3/8" (1 cm) -long teardrop. Make five cuts in the upper part of the clay. Spread each piece apart with the modeling tool.

4. Insert the wire of the flower center from step 2 from above through the bottom of the flower. Apply glue to the inside bottom of the flower center and secure it. Make fifteen of them, making a mix of open and closed flowers. Let them dry completely.

5. Make the bud. Roll a ⅛" (3 mm) ball of light green clay into a ¼" (6 mm) -long teardrop. Apply glue to the hook of the wire and insert it into the bottom of the clay. Make eighteen buds and let them dry completely.

2. Make the leaves
Cut the No.26 wire into six and wrap them with narrow tape. Prepare eighteen.

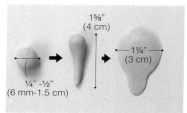

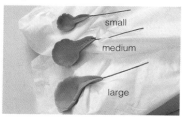

1. Roll a ⅜"-⅝" (6 mm-1.5 cm) ball of green clay into a 1⅝" (4 cm) -long, bulb-like teardrop. Place the clay on the pressing mat and flatten it until it is 1¼" (3 cm) wide. Stretch the edge with your finger to make it thinner. Gently press the modeling tool into eight or so places around the edges to make notches.

2. Apply glue to the tip of the wire and attach it to the leaf center. Pinch the edges of both sides to secure to clay. Bend the bottom of the leaf downward. Make eighteen of them in a range of small, medium, and large sizes. For the large leaf, drape the leaf over the edge of a tissue-covered foam block to dry.

3. Paint and assemble the flowers
Place a small amount of each color on a plastic-wrapped paint palette or work surface.

Mix a base coat of pink and white for the flower. Paint the middle part of the flower with peony. Paint the bud with sage green mixed with green. Mix a base coat of sage green and green for the leaf. Paint a few dark green details on the leaves. Paint white along the edge of the leaves then highlight it with purple mixed with brown. For the flower and bud, gather three to four together then attach to the tip of the No. 18 wire with narrow floral tape. Arrange leaves from small to large size in a downward spiral, facing them downward. Make two branches.

Spring

Lily of the Valley

MATERIALS (for three flowers)

Resin clay:
Flower center, bud, open flower: 1" (2.5 cm) ball
Leaf, furled leaf: 1¾" (4.5 cm) ball

Floral wire:
No. 26 5: bud stem, flower
No. 20 4: leaf stem, stem for assembly

Floral tape: Light green (narrow)

Oil paint: white, green, dark green, grass green, blue

Prepare the clay

flower center, bud, open flower — 1" (2.5 cm)

leaf, furled leaf — 1¾" (4.5 cm)

For the flower center, bud, and open flower, add a small amount of white to a 1" (2.5 cm) ball of white clay.

For the leaf and furled leaf, add equal amounts of green and dark green to a 1¾" (4.5 cm) ball of white clay to make green.

1. Make the flower center, bud, and open flower

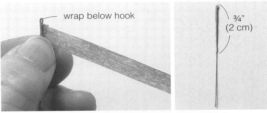

wrap below hook

¾" (2 cm)

1. Cut the No. 26 wire into six equal pieces. Make a hook in one end of each. Starting just below the hook, wrap ¾" (2 cm) of each piece with floral tape. Make twenty-six.

2. Make the flower center. Apply glue to the hook and insert the hook end of the wire into a 1/8" (3 mm) ball of white clay. Make four cuts into the top of the clay then close them again with your fingers. Let dry completely. Make twenty.

Make the flower center, bud, and open flower *(continued)*

3. Make the bud. Apply glue to the hook and insert the hook end of the wire into a 1/4" (6 mm) ball of white clay. Make four cuts into the top of the clay then close them again with your fingers. Make three small ones, then make three larger ones, starting with slightly larger balls of clay.

4. Make the open flower. Roll a ⅜" (1 cm) ball of white clay. Make six cuts into the top of the clay.

5. Gently lift each piece of clay from the center with a thin modeling tool. Be careful not to spread the pieces apart. Reshape the inside hollow with the thicker end of the modeling tool. The finished flower shape should be hollow and balloon-like.

6. Insert the wire of the flower center through the middle of the open flower. Apply glue to the inside bottom of the flower center to secure it to the petals. Bend the petals so they open outward.

7. Following steps 4-6, make about thirty in varying sizes (see finished flower photo, page 110. One branch has seven to ten buds and flowers). Insert them into the foam block and let dry completely.

2. Make the leaves
Wrap the No. 20 wire with narrow floral tape. Cut in three equal pieces for the medium and large leaves. Prepare six. Cut in four equal pieces for the furled leaf. Make a hook in one end and prepare three.

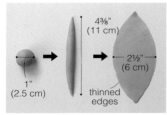

1. Make the large leaf. Roll a 1" (2.5 cm) ball of green clay into a 4⅜" (11 cm) -long tube with pointed ends. Place the clay on the pressing mat and flatten it until it is 2½" (6 cm) wide. Stretch the edge with your fingers to make it thinner.

2. Turn over the leaf and make frills along the edge by rolling the modeling tool.

3. Turn over the leaf again and add long, textured lines into the surface with the brush end of a quilter's pencil.

4. Draw a line at the center of the leaf with rolling cutter.

5. Apply glue along the top third of a leaf wire and affix it to the lower third of the leaf. Pinch the leaf from behind to secure it to the clay. Make three large leaves. For the medium leaf, start with a smaller ball of green clay. Make three medium-sized leaves.

6. Make the furled leaf. Roll a ¾" (2 cm) ball of green clay into a 2¾"-3⅛" (7-7.75 cm) -long tube. Place the clay on the pressing mat and flatten it until it is 1⅝"-2" (4-5 cm) wide. Stretch the edge with your finger to make it thinner. Repeat steps 2-4 to add the leaf details. Curl both sides of the leaf inward.

glue

7. Apply glue to the hook of a No. 20 wire and insert it 1" (2.5 cm) into the bottom of the leaf and affix it. Make three.

furled leaf

8. Place tissue paper over the foam block and lay the leaves over it to let them dry completely.

3. Paint the flowers and leaves

Place a small amount of each color on a plastic-wrapped paint palette or work surface.

1. Paint a white base coat on the open flowers and buds. Paint the center of the open flower lightly with grass green. Paint the bottom of the open flower and bud very lightly with grass green, brushing bottom to top.

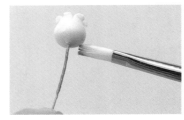

2. Over the first coat, paint green details on the bottom of the open flower and bud.

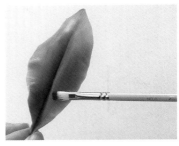

3. Paint a green base coat on the leaf and rolled leaf (front and back sides). Paint the middle to lower section with blue mixed with green. Paint the back side lightly, too. Paint a light white line along the center leaf vein.

3. Assemble the flower

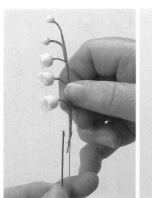

1. Wrap the small-bud stem with floral tape (starting from below the bud). Affix a large bud ½" (1.5 cm) below the small bud, leaving a ⅜" (1 cm) stem. Curve the stem of the open flower and affix it ½" (1.5 cm) below the bud, leaving a ⅜" (1 cm) stem. Wrap the main stem with tape. After adding three flowers with only tape, attach a length of No. 20 wire (cut in thirds). Wrap the wire and stem with tape. Attach two through five open flowers to the wire in the same manner as before. Wrap the entire stem neatly with tape, trying not to thicken the upper part of the stem.

2. Hold the medium-sized and furled leaves together and tape them together at the stem bottoms. Place them alongside the flower stem (from step 1) and wrap the stems together with floral tape. Place the large leaf slightly below the other leaves, and at the opposite side, and wrap the stems with tape. Wrap one more time to finish the stems.

Spring

Anemone

MATERIALS (for two flowers)

Resin clay:
Petal: 2" (5 cm) ball
Flower center: ¾" (2 cm) ball
Leaf: 1⅝" (4 cm) ball

Floral wire:
No. 22 2: (leaf stem)
No. 16 2: (flower stem)

Floral tape: Light green (narrow and regular width)

Oil paint: green, dark green, blue, purple, black, white

Rose pips: one bunch (flower center)

Prepare the clay

For the flower center, add a bit of black to ¾"
(2 cm) ball of white clay to make black.
For the leaf, add green and dark green to a
1⅝" (4 cm) ball of white clay to make light
green.

1. Make center of flower

Instructions are given for one flower

*Wrap the No. 16 wire with regular-width tape and make a
hook in one end.*

1. Roll a ⅜" (1 cm) ball of black
clay. Apply glue to the hook of
the wire and insert it into the
ball. Pinch the base of the
clay to secure it to the wire.

2. Starting from the middle of
the flower center, make small
V shape cuts in the clay surface
with scissors. Make randomly
placed cuts across the entire
surface. Let dry completely.

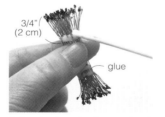

3 Cut the bunch of rose pips in
two (each half is used for each
side of the flower center). Paint
the pip stems purple and the
tips black. Apply glue ¾" (2 cm)
below the tips of both halves.

4. After the glue has dried halfway, cut the pips ¾" (2 cm) from
the tips. Apply glue to the bottom
of the pips. Attach the two sets of
pips around the flower center.

5. Wrap 3" (7.5 cm) of the stem, starting
from the base of the pistil/stamen, with tissue paper. Wrap over the tissue twice with
regular width tape. Burnish the surface of
the tape with the side of the pliers to make
it shiny. The flower center is complete.

2. Make and assemble the petals

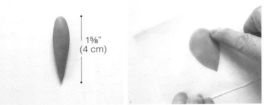

1. Make the inner petal. Roll a ⅜" (1 cm) ball of blue-purple clay into a 1⅝" (4 cm) -long teardrop. Place the clay on the pressing mat and flatten it until it is 1" wide. Stretch the edge with your finger to make it thinner.

2. Add frills to the petal edges with your fingers.

3. Press the petal with the tapered modeling tool at the frills to imprint lines at the edges.

4. Pinch the petal center from the back side to crease slightly.

5. Place the petal on your palm. Press the petal center with the ball end of a rounded modeling tool, rolling from bottom to top to round the petal.

6. Make four of them. Place them on rolled tissue paper nests while you make the outer petal.

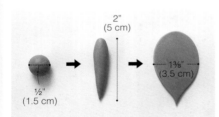

7. Make the outer petal. Roll a ½" (1.5 cm) ball of blue-purple clay into a 2" (5 cm) -long teardrop. Place the clay on the pressing mat and flatten it until it is 1⅜" (3.5 cm) wide and follow steps 2-6. Make eight.

8. After the petals have dried halfway, apply glue to the bottom of twelve petals. Place four inner petals around the center of flower and affix them so they cover the bottom of the flower center. Affix four outer petals between the inner petals.

9. Affix the remaining four outer petals between the first round of outer petals. Insert the stem through the center the petals, nestling it against a flat "platform", allowing room for the flower center. Reshape the petals as desired and place it in a vase to dry completely.

3. Make the leaf
Wrap the No. 22 wire with narrow tape and cut into four equal pieces. Prepare three (for one branch).

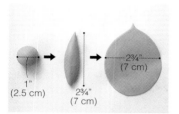

1. Roll a 1" (2.5 cm) ball of light green into a 2¾" (7 cm) -long teardrop. Place the clay on the pressing mat and flatten it until it is 2¾" (7 cm) wide. Stretch the edge with your finger to make it thinner.

2. Place the template (below) on the clay from step 1 and trace the pattern with a bamboo stick. Place the leaf over the strawberry leaf mold to make an imprint of the leaf veins.

3. Turn it over. Roll the modeling tool along the edge to make it thinner. Apply glue to one-third of the wire and affix it to the center leaf vein. Pinch the leaf from the back side to secure it. Make three. Let dry for 24 hours.

4. Paint and assemble the flower
Place a small amount of each color on a plastic-wrapped paint palette or work surface.

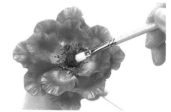

1. Paint a base coat of purple mixed with blue to the top side of the petal, but do not paint the base of the petals. Paint a light base coat on the back side. Add blue to the same brush and paint the edges and base of the petals lightly to add detail.

2. Paint the inside base of the petals white.

3. Paint the outside base of the petals white, brushing from bottom to top. Then mix purple and green to make brown, and paint the top of the stem up to the bottom of the petals.

4. Paint the flower center and tip of pips black.

5. Paint a base coat of green on the leaf, and paint a light coat on the back. Paint the leaf edge and center lightly with dark green to add detail, then paint the bottom of the leaf white. Paint a white line along the center leaf vein. Paint the bottom of leaf lightly with purple.

6. Assemble the flower. Place a leaf at 2"-2¾" (5-7 cm) below the bottom of the flower. Wrap 3/4" (2 cm) of the step with narrow tape. Repeat for the other two leaves, taping them in place one at a time. Wrap the stem with tissue paper, then wrap the tissue with three layers of regular width tape to make it thicker. Burnish the tape with the side of the pliers to make it shiny. Make two.

Leaf template (actual size)

BOUQUET

White Star Bouquet

MATERIALS (for bouquet)

Resin clay:
Flower, bud, pistil: 1¾" (4.5 cm) ball
Calyx, stamen: 1 1/4" (3 cm) ball
Leaf: 1¾" (4.5 cm) ball

Floral wire:
No. 24 16: flower, leaf
No. 18 1: for the handle

Floral tape: Light green (narrow and regular width)

Faux flower stamens (or floral pips): 3 packages/bunches

Oil paint: green, dark green, sage green, white

Prepare the clay

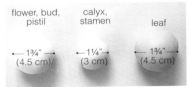

flower, bud, pistil — 1¾" (4.5 cm)
calyx, stamen — 1¼" (3 cm)
leaf — 1¾" (4.5 cm)

For the flower, bud, and pistil, add a bit of white to a 1¾" (4.5 cm) ball of white clay.

For the calyx and stamen, add a bit of dark green to a 1¼" (3 cm) ball of white clay to make light green.

For the leaf, add dark green and green to a 1¾" (4.5 cm) ball of white clay to make green.

1. Make the flower and the small bud

*Wrap the No. 24 wire with narrow tape and cut in four equal pieces. Make hook in one end. Prepare fifty.

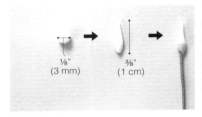

1. Make the pistil. Roll a ⅛" (3 mm) ball of white clay into a ⅜" (1 cm) -long teardrop. Apply glue to the hook of the wire and insert it into the thicker end of the teardrop. Make thirty.

⅛" (3 mm)   ⅜" (1 cm)

2. Make the stamen. Roll a ¼" (6 mm) ball of light green clay into a ⅜" (1 cm) -long teardrop. Make a hole in the thicker end of the teardrop by rolling the bamboo stick back and forth. Make five ⅛" (3 mm) cuts into the edge.

3. Insert the wire of the pistil through the center of the stamen. Apply glue to the bottom of the pistil and secure it in place. Close the tips of the stamen with your fingers. Make thirty and let them dry completely in the foam block.

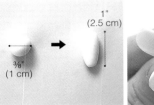

4. Make the open flower. Roll a ⅜" (1 cm) ball of white clay into a 1" (2.5 cm) -long oval shape (with one end slightly thicker). Cut the thicker end into five pieces. Spread each piece apart and widen them to make the petals. Round the petal ends.

5. Insert the wire of the flower center through the petals. Apply glue to the bottom of the stamen and secure them in place. Make thirty total, a mix of open and closed flowers.

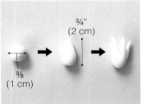

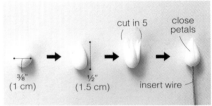

6. Make the half-open flower. Roll a ⅜" (1 cm) ball of white clay into a ¾" (2 cm) -long teardrop. Cut the pointed end into five equal pieces and spread them apart with the modeling tool. Pinch the tips of the petals with your fingers so they are pointed.

7. Close the petals organically. Apply glue to the hook of a No. 24 wire (as prepared for a flower center) and insert it into the base. Make twelve.

8. Make the bud. Roll a ⅜" (1 cm) ball of white clay into a ½" (1.5 cm) -long teardrop. Cut the pointed end into five pieces, then close them with your fingers. Apply glue to the hook of a No. 24 wire and insert it into the base. Make eight.

2. Make and attach the calyx

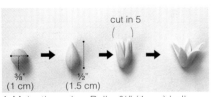

1. Make the calyx. Roll a ⅜" (1 cm) ball of light green clay into a ½" (1.5 cm) long teardrop. Cut the pointed end into five pieces. Spread the five pieces with the modeling tool.

2. Insert the wire of the open flower (or the half-open flower and bud) into calyx. Apply glue to the outside bottom of flower. Arrange the flower so the points of the calyx are between the petals. Let dry completely.

3. Make the leaf

Wrap the No. 24 wire with narrow floral tape, and cut into four equal pieces. Prepare twelve.

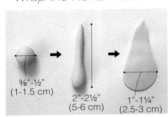  

1. Roll a ⅜"-½" (1-1.5 cm) ball into a 2"-2½" (5-6 cm) -long teardrop with a fat base. Place the clay on the pressing mat and flatten it until it is 1"-1¼" (2.5-3 cm) wide. Press it on the strawberry leaf mold to imprint the leaf veins. Cut a V shape at the leaf base. Turn it over. Roll the modeling tool along the edge make frills.

2. Apply glue to two-thirds of the wire and place it along to center leaf vein. Pinch the leaf from the back side to secure the wire. Make twelve leaves total in a range of sizes. Let the leaves dry completely on tissue laid over the foam block.

4. Painting the flower and leaves

Place a small amount of each color on a plastic-wrapped paint palette or work surface.

1. Paint the open flower. Paint a white base coat on the petals. Lightly paint the back white. Lightly paint the stamen with sage green, and paint the bottom of the petals green.

2. Mix sage green and green and paint the calyx, brushing from bottom to top. Let the color fade as you approach the top. Paint the closed flower the same way.

3. Paint a white base coat on the half-open flower and bud. Lightly paint the tip of the bud green. Paint the calyx in the same manner as the open flower.

4. Paint a sage green base coat on the leaf. Lightly paint the back. Paint part of the leaf with sage green mixed with green. Paint a white line at the leaf center.

To assemble the bouquet:

Gather two or three bundles of buds and tape their stems together. Place a small pansy (see page 54) as the center, and wrap the stems of all flowers together. Arrange the leaves around the flowers and wrap the wire stems with tape. Wrap the entire bundle with one even layer of floral tape it and tie a decorative ribbon around it.

ACCESSORIES
Anemone Pin

Prepare the clay

For the flower center, add dark green to ⅜" (1 cm) ball of clay to make light green.

For the petals, add a bit of white to a 1" (2.5 cm) ball of clay to make white.

For the leaf, add a bit of dark green to a 1" (2.5 cm) ball of clay to make green-tinted white.

See page 113 for the actual-size leaf template

MATERIALS (for two flowers)

Resin clay:
Petal: 2" (5 cm) ball
Flower center: ¾" (2 cm) ball
Leaf: 1⅝" (4 cm) ball

Floral wire:
No. 22 2: (leaf stem)
No. 16 2: (flower stem)

Floral tape: Light green (narrow and regular width)

Oil paint: green, dark green, blue, purple, black, white

Rose pips: one bunch (flower center)

1. Make center of flower

Follow all instructions for the flower center, petal, and leaf for the Anemone, page 111.

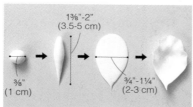

1⅜"-2"
(3.5-5 cm)

⅜"
(1 cm)

¾"-1¼"
(2-3 cm)

1. Make small and large petals. Roll a ⅜" (1 cm) ball of white clay into a 1⅜"-2" (3.5-5 cm) -long teardrop. Place the clay on the pressing mat and flatten it until it is ¾" -1¼" (2-3 cm) wide and petal-shaped. Make twelve and let them dry completely.

2. Make the flower center (see page 111), painting the rose pips dark green. Attach the pips to the flower center. Attach the petals around the flower center. Flip the flower over. Trim the back side of the flower to create a flat surface for the pin back. Place it on a curved aluminum foil platform to dry. The clay will dry clear.

3. Apply a thick layer of glue to the pin base and attach it to a large leaf.

4. Apply glue to the back of the flower made in step 2. Apply glue to the leaf then attach the flower to the leaf.

5. Let the finished flower pin dry completely. Add glitter to the edges of the petals to finish it.

ACCESSORIES

Camellia Necklace & Earrings

AMAZING CLAY FLOWERS

MATERIALS

Resin clay (clear):
Open flower, bud: 1¼" (3 cm) ball
Leaf: 1¼" (3 cm)

Oil paint: dark green

Necklace base: 1

Earring base: 1 pair

Pearl beads: 4

Aurora flower pips: half bunch (flower center for pin);
10 (flower center for earrings)

Silver Glitter

Prepare the clay

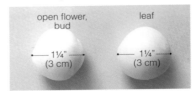

For the open flower and bud, use a 1¼" (3 cm) ball of clay as is.
For the leaf, add a bit of dark green to a 1¼" (3 cm) ball of clay to make green-tinted white.

NECKLACE

1. Make the flower center

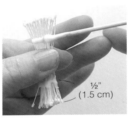

1. Apply glue ½" (1.5 cm) from both ends (the tips) of the half-bunch of flower peps. Apply glue to both front and back sides.

2. After the glue is half dry, cut the peps just below the glue (one for each of the two open flowers).

2. Make the petal and bud

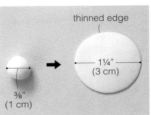

1. Make the petal. Roll a ⅜" (1 cm) ball of clear clay into a 1¼" (3 cm) -wide circle. Stretch the upper edge with your finger to make it thinner.

2. Press and roll the tapered modeling tool against the clay to imprint lines.

3. Pinch the center of the petal from the back side. Place the petal in your palm, then roll the rounded modeling tool along the center crease to shape the petal.

4. Bend the upper part of the petal to the outside. Make ten. Let the petals dry halfway.

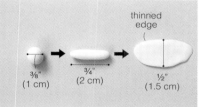

thinned edge

⅜"
(1 cm)

¾"
(2 cm)

½"
(1.5 cm)

5. Make the bud. Roll a ⅜" (1 cm) ball of clear clay into a ¾" (2 cm) -long tube. Place the clay on the pressing mat and flatten it until it is ½" (1.5 cm) wide. Stretch the upper edge with your finger to make it thinner. Use the tapered modeling tool to add waves to the upper edge.

6. Turn over the clay. Roll the widened upper half outward. Make three and let them dry completely on individual tissue nests.

3. Assemble the flower

Apply glue to the bottom of each petal and affix them to the flower center. Overlap the second petal over the first one, and place the third petal between the first and the second. The other two petals are affixed below the first three. Make two.

4. Make the necklace

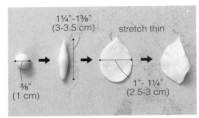

1. Make the leaf. Roll a ⅜" (1 cm) ball of green-tinted clay into a 1¼"-1⅜" (3-3.5 cm) long tapered teardrop. Place the clay on the pressing mat and flatten it until it is 1"- 1¼" (2.5-3 cm) wide. Stretch the upper tip with your finger to make it thinner. Imprint leaf veins with a modeling tool. Press a center line in the leaf with scissors. Fold the leaf in half from the back side. Make eight.

2. Scratch the inside of the necklace base with pliers.

3. Apply a layer of glue to the inside of the necklace base. Fill the base with a crescent-shaped green-tinted white clay.

4. Before the clay dries, apply glue to the bottom of the back of the leaf. Attach the smaller leaves at the sides and the larger leaves at the center.

5. Trim the back side of the flower to create a flat surface. Apply glue to the back side and affix it to the leaves. Place two flowers at an angle. Affix three buds around the flowers.

6. Apply glue to the base, and attach four pearl beads. Let the necklace dry.

7. Once the clay has dried clear, add glitter to the edges of the flowers and in other places to finish the necklace.

EARRINGS

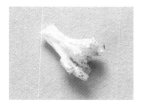

1. Add glue to ten flower pips and cut in two (following the instructions for the flower center).

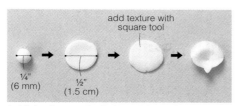

2. Make the petals. Roll a ¼" (6 mm) ball of clay and press it flat into a ½" (1.5 cm) -wide circle. Make ten (in the same manner as the necklace). Let them dry halfway.

3. Attach five petals around the center of flower.

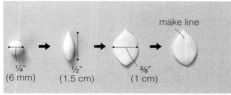

4. For the leaf, roll a ¼" (6 mm) ball of clay into a ½" (1.5 cm) -long teardrop. Place the clay on the pressing mat and flatten it until it is ⅜" (1 cm) wide. Imprint a line along the center. Make four.

5. Scratch the earring base with pliers, and apply a thick layer of glue. Affix two leaves (do not let them dry) to the earring bases.

6. Trim the back side of the flower to create a flat surface. Glue to the flowers to the earring bases. Add glitter to the flowers after it dries completely.

ᗩCCESSORIES

Rose Basket Pin & Earrings

MATERIALS (for bouquet)

Resin clay (clear):
Center of flower, bud, open flower: 1" (2.5 cm) ball
Setaria: 1/2" (1.5 cm) ball
Leaf: 3/4" (2 cm) ball

Floral wire:
No. 26 2: leaf stem
No. 24 1: bud stem, open flower

Floral tape: Light green (narrow and regular width)

Faux flower stamens (or floral pips): 3 packages/bunches

Oil paint: green, dark green, grass green, white

Acrylic color: cold

Nylon thread: 10" (25 cm) (for setaria stem)

Pin base: 1

Earring base: 1 pair

Prepare the clay

For the flower center, bud, and open flower, add a bit of white to a 1" (2.5 cm) ball of clay to make white.

For the setaria, add a bit of green to a ½" (1.5 cm) ball of clay to make green-tinted white.

For the leaf, add a bit of dark green to a ¾" (2 cm) ball of clay to make light green.

PIN

1. Make the open flower and bud
Cut the No. 24 wire into two 1⅝" (4 cm) -long pieces. Make a hook in one end of each wire.

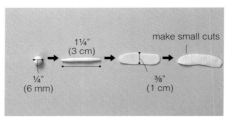

1. Make the flower center for the open flower. Roll a ¼" (6 mm) ball of white clay into a 1¼" (3 cm) -long tube. Press it flat until it is ⅜" (1 cm) wide. Stretch the upper edge with your finger to make it thinner. Make cuts every ⅛" (3 mm) along the upper edge, cutting a little over halfway across the shape.

2. Apply glue to the hook of the wire and attach it to the left corner of the clay shape. Wrap the clay around the hook. Let the clay dry completely.

3. Make the bud center. Insert the glued wire into the bottom of a ¼" (6 mm) ball of white clay. Pinch the base of the clay to secure it. Let it dry completely.

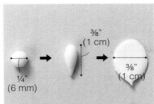

4. Make the inner petal. Roll a ¼" (6 mm) ball of white clay into a ⅜" (1 cm) -long teardrop. Place the clay on the pressing mat and flatten it until it is ⅜" (1 cm) wide.

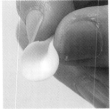
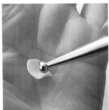

5. Pinch the petal from the back side and fold it in half. Place it on your palm and round the center with the rounded modeling tool. Pinch the tip of the petal. Make three. Let the petals dry halfway.

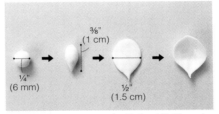

6. Make the outer petals. Roll a ¼" (6 mm) ball of white clay into a ⅜" (1 cm) -long teardrop. Press it flat until it is ½" (1.5 cm) wide. Follow step 5 above to shape the petal. Make three. Let the petals dry halfway.

7. Assemble the pin. Apply glue to the bottom of six petals. Attach three inner petals so they wrap around the flower center.

8. Attach three outer petals, placing them between the inner petals. Let them dry.

9. Make the bud. Make three petals that are smaller than the inner petal of open flower. Apply glue to the bottom of the petal and attach them so they wrap around the bud center from step 3. Let dry completely.

2. Make the setaria

Cut six 1⅝" (4 cm) long pieces of nylon thread.

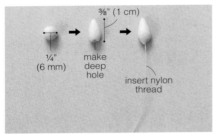  

1. Roll a ¼" (6 mm) ball of green-tinted clay into a ⅜" (1 cm) -long teardrop. Make a deep hole in the bottom of the clay with a toothpick. Apply glue to the tip of the nylon thread and insert it into the clay. Pinch the bottom of clay to secure the thread.

2. Hold the clay with the tip facing down and make V shaped cuts with the tip of the scissors from bottom to top. Make six and let them dry completely.

3. Make the leaf

Cut the No. 26 wire into eleven 1¼" (3 cm) -long pieces.

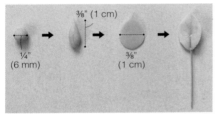 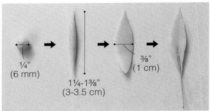

1. Make the rose leaf. Roll a ¼" (6 mm) ball of light green clay into a ⅜" (1 cm) -long teardrop. Place the clay on the pressing mat and flatten it until it is ⅜" (1 cm) wide. Imprint lines at the center and radiating outward from the center. Apply glue to the tip of wire and press it along the center of the leaf. Pinch the leaf from the back side and secure the wire. Make five and let them dry completely.

2. Make the setaria leaf. Roll a ¼" (6 mm) ball of light green clay into a 1¼-1⅜" (3-3.5 cm) -long tube with both ends pointed. Press it flat until it is ⅜" (1 cm) wide. Imprint a line along the center of the leaf. Apply glue to the tip of the wire and attach it along the center line. Pinch the leaf from the back side to secure the wire. Make six and let them dry completely.

4. Assemble the pin

Cut the wire for the flower and leaf to the length you like. Apply glue to the tip of wire and insert it into the clay.

1. Roll a ⅜" (1 cm) ball of light green clay into a small tube. Apply glue into the open part of the pin base and fill with the clay.

2. Affix a ⅜" (1 cm) ball of light green clay to the back of pin base with glue. Be careful not to cover the pin.

3. Place the open flower and the bud into the basket. Cut the wire of the open flower. Insert the wire into the clay and glue. Repeat for the bud, placed beside the flower.

AMAZING CLAY FLOWERS

4. Attach five rose leaves around the flower.

5. Attach six setaria leaves around the arrangement.

6. To add the setaria, first make a hole with a toothpick in the clay base. Apply glue to one end of the nylon threads. Insert the nylon thread into the clay.

7. Roll a ball of light green clay into a wide tube. Apply glue and affix it to the back to support all the clay parts. Let dry completely.

8. Paint the flowers and leaves: Paint a light coat of grass green at the bottom of the flower center, flower, and bud. Paint gold spots along the edges of the leaves and the setaria.

ROSE BASKET PIN & EARRINGS

Tips for assembling the earrings:

Prepare two rose leaves and one open flower. Attach the leaves then the open flower to each earring base. Make a second earring.

Acknowledgments

Thank you to the entire publishing team, who has worked so tirelessly to make this lovely book a dream come true. I'd like to thank specifically Takeo Nakano, publisher of Oshare Kobo; editor-in-chief Chikami Okuda; editor Satomi Ochiai; photographer Itsuji Tsushima; stylist Terumi Inoue, and book designer Ami Sudo.

About the Author

Noriko Kawaguchi was born in Tokyo, but she has lived in Kuala Lumpur, Singapore, and London, where she studied arts and crafts. She teaches and exhibits her work both in Japan and internationally. She is the author of several craft books on working with art clay and resin clay.